Living with a Greyhound

Edited by Cynthia Branigan

BARRON'S

THE QUESTION OF GENDER

The* he *pronoun is used throughout this book in favor of the rather impersonal* it*, but no gender bias is intended at all.

ACKNOWLEDGEMENTS

The publisher would like to thank the following for help with photography: The Retired Greyhound Trust, Make Peace With Animals, Tony Meek, Mandie Taylor, Alex Whissen, and Greyhound Rescue West of England.

First edition for the United States and Canada published by Barron's Educational Series, Inc., 2001

All inquiries should be addressed to:
Barron's Educational Series, Inc.
250 Wireless Boulevard
Hauppauge, New York 11788
http://www.barronseduc.com

Library of Congress Catalog Card No. 2001093443

International Standard Book No. 0-7641-5428-1

Printed in Singapore

9 8 7 6 5 4 3 2 1

CONTENTS

1 INTRODUCING THE GREYHOUND 7

The sighthound family; The coursing Greyhound; Track racing; The modern Greyhound; The show Greyhound; The companion Greyhound.

2 UNDERSTANDING RACING DOGS 15

Breeding a racing Greyhound; Racing career; Racing injuries; Retirement.

3 ADOPTING A GREYHOUND 27

The pros; The cons; Great expectations; Lifestyles; Rehoming prospects; First contact; Adoption agencies; The adoption process; Greyhounds and other animals; Greyhounds and children; Signing up; Preparing for the new arrival; Preparing your home.

4 SETTLING IN 47

Collecting your Greyhound; Arriving home; Meeting the family; The resident dog; Meeting the cat; Encounters with small animals; House-training; The first meal; The first night; House rules; The outside world; Leaving your Greyhound; Establishing a routine; The settled Greyhound.

5 CARING FOR YOUR GREYHOUND 65
Feeding; Grooming; Temperature control; Exercising your Greyhound; The aging Greyhound; Letting go.

6 TRAINING TARGETS 79
Starting right; Training exercises; Training classes; Solving problems; The destructive Greyhound; Inappropriate toileting; The macho Greyhound; The aggressive Greyhound; The dominant Greyhound; The timid Greyhound; Seeking help.

7 HAVING FUN WITH YOUR GREYHOUND 97
Canine Good Citizen; Public relations and fund-raising; Artificial lure coursing; Agility; Therapy dogs.

8 HEALTH CARE 107
General health care; Vaccination; Internal parasites; External parasites; Teeth care; Eyes; Ears; Skin conditions; Digestive problems; Diabetes; Arthritis; Epilepsy; Heart disease; Summary.

CHAPTER ONE

INTRODUCING THE GREYHOUND

Beautiful and athletic, with a sweetness of temperament that is second to none, the Greyhound has a very special place in our affections. All too often, the dog-loving fraternity is swayed by a cute little puppy, but the Greyhound is probably the one exception to this. Greyhound puppies are certainly sweet, but most Greyhound owners fall in love with the adult, and, in the vast majority of cases, they take on a fully grown dog.

This is because the Greyhound, the athlete of the canine world, is very much a working dog. Greyhound racing is a hugely popular sport, and the industry demands many thousands of dogs to compete at tracks in the United States, the UK, and Ireland. However, most Greyhounds are ready to retire at three or four years of age, and then they must start a new chapter in their lives – living as companion dogs.

For the purposes of this book, we are looking at the retired Greyhound, trying to understand how his mind works, how to care for him, and how to provide the best possible life for him in his new home.

THE SIGHTHOUND FAMILY

The Greyhound is a member of the sighthound family, and, as the name implies, it is made up of dogs that hunt primarily by sight rather than by scent. Better-known sighthounds include the Afghan Hound, the Saluki, and the Whippet, plus the more obscure Chart Polski (Polish Greyhound) and the Magyar Agar (Hungarian Greyhound).

The origins of the different sighthound breeds vary, but their roots go back to ancient civilization. There is evidence of Greyhound-like dogs depicted on a temple wall in Turkey, which dates back to 6000 B.C.E. It is a hunting scene that shows dogs with long legs and deep chests in pursuit of their quarry. In Ancient Egypt, the Greyhound held an honored place in many households, and it was said that the

The spectacular sight of a Greyhound at full stretch.

death of a Greyhound was second only in importance to the death of a son. Drawings of sleek hunting dogs, working closely with their human owners, are seen in many Egyptian tombs.

The sight of a Greyhound running at full speed, twisting and turning his athletic body, has thrilled crowds for literally thousands of years. In Ancient Greece, the sport of coursing, where two Greyhounds were set loose in pursuit of a hare, became a popular pastime.

But it was when the Greyhound became a favorite of the Romans that his fame spread. The Greyhound was highly prized as a companion as well as a hunting dog, and, when the empire spread to Britain and Ireland, Greyhounds also made the journey.

It is thought that the first Greyhounds made their way to North America when Christopher Columbus led expeditions to the New World. But the major influx came in the 1800s when many British and Irish settlers came to live in the Midwest and western states.

THE COURSING GREYHOUND

The development of a breed depends entirely on the work it has to do. The best workers are bred from, and the best physical features are sought after.

In the ancient civilizations of the Middle East, sighthounds hunted in hot, often desert-like conditions. In order to run at top speed, they needed long legs, a deep chest to accommodate a big heart and plenty of lung room, and a fine coat so that they did not become overheated.

In addition, they needed excellent vision so that they could spot their quarry on the horizon.

When the Greyhound came to Britain and Ireland, it quickly found fame as both a hunting and a coursing dog. Ownership was restricted to the nobility – and so the breed had a highly privileged status.

Money was no object, and every effort was made to improve the breed. Edmund de Langley, a son of King Edward III, wrote in the 1370s:

The Greihound should have a long hede and somedele grete, ymaked in the manner of a luce; a good large mouth and good sessours, the one again the other, so that the nether jaws passe not them above, ne that thei above passe not him neither.

The neck should be grete and longe, and bowed as a swannne's neck.

Her shuldres as a roebuck; the for leggs streght ynow, and nought to hind legges; the feet straught and round as a catte, and great cleas; the boones and joyntes of the cheyne grete and hard as the chyne of an hert; the thighs great and squarred as an hare; the houghs streight and not crompyng as of an oxe.

A catte's tayle, making a ring at eend, but not to hie.

Coursing as a purely competitive sport grew in popularity in Tudor times, and a code was drawn up for judging the winner of coursing stakes. The hotbed of coursing was the east of England. In 1776, the Earl of Orford, known as the creator of modern coursing, founded the first public coursing club in Swaffham, Norfolk.

Lord Orford was a great British eccentric; his favorite mode of transport was a carriage drawn by four stags, but he was in deadly earnest when it came to breeding Greyhounds for coursing. His mission was to create the perfect Greyhound, and he experimented with a number of crosses with other breeds, such as Lurchers, Italian Greyhounds, and even Bulldogs. At one time, Lord Orford kept over a

The British were great coursing enthusiasts.

hundred Greyhounds, and his expenditure was so high that he was forced to sell the family's collection of paintings to Catherine the Great of Russia.

His greatest dog was Czarina, who won 47 matches without loss. It is said that Lord Orford watched Czarina defeat her rival Maria on Newmarket Heath. He raised his hat to the bitch – and died.

Czarina was sold to Colonel Thomas Thornton, and, at the advanced age of 13, she whelped her first litter. It included a dog called Claret who went on to sire the great Snowball, winner of four cups and over 30 matches.

Snowball, who was, in fact, a black dog, was immortalized in verse by Sir Walter Scott:

> "Twas when fleet Snowball's head was waxen grey,
> A luckless lev'ret met him on his way;
> Who knows not Snowball? He whose race renowned
> Is still victorious on each coursing ground.
> Swaffham, Newmarket and the Roman Camp
> Have seen them victors o'er each meaner stamp.
> In vain the youngling sought with doubling wile
> The hedge, the hill, the thicket or the stile,
> Experience sage the lack of speed supplied,
> And in the gap he sought, – the victim died."

As the sport developed, the most successful dogs on the field, such as King Cob, winner of the Newmarket Cup and the St. Leger, were used at public stud. Detailed records of pedigrees were kept, and, eventually, in 1882, a Greyhound Stud Book was established.

Coursing enjoyed its heyday in the Victorian era, when meetings were attended by huge crowds. As the sport demanded more Greyhounds of the highest caliber, the breed was perfected as the supreme canine athlete.

TRACK RACING

The true coursing enthusiast saw the introduction of park coursing in 1876 as the end of the Greyhound's reign. This was a course that was run in an enclosed "park" over a distance of 800 yards instead of the three-mile open course of the traditional meetings. Obviously, the Greyhound's speed was at a premium, and stamina became far less significant.

However, events taking place in the United States had a far greater impact. Coursing was illegal in many states in the United States, and so the invention of an easy-to-operate, artificial lure was viewed with great interest. Owen Patrick Smith demonstrated the first lure of this type at Hot Springs, South Dakota, in 1905, and in 1919 he had his own racetrack – in Emeryville, CA – and it was an instant success. Within six years, Smith was the owner of 25 tracks, and is justly known as the founder of modern racing.

News of the sport spread to Britain, and, on July 24, 1926, Mistley became the first

Born in the United States, track racing soon took Britain by storm.

winner of a Greyhound race in England. The meeting was held at Belle Vue Stadium, Manchester.

The challenge of Greyhounds racing around a track, rather than being let loose on a straight course, added more chance and excitement to the race, and it was a bonus that meetings could be held at night under floodlights. Within six months, crowds of 17,000 were thronging to Belle Vue, and new tracks were opening up all over Britain. Ireland followed the trend, and soon tracks were opened in Belfast and then in Dublin. A year after racing arrived in Britain, a track was opened in Harold Park, Australia. Greyhound racing had become an instant, international success.

THE MODERN GREYHOUND

The demands of track racing were soon found to be very different from the rigors of the coursing field, and, as a result, a different type of Greyhound has emerged.

The track Greyhound is trained to race over distances ranging from 218 to 765 yards (200 to 700 meters). The race time will range between 15 and 40 seconds. Greyhounds also compete in hurdle races and in some marathon races that may cover 1,094 yards (1,000 meters) and last over 60 seconds. Since the inception of track racing, breeding has concentrated on refining the Greyhound's natural sprinting ability, increasing strength and stamina, and producing an animal that has the highly competitive mental attitude of a top athlete.

Like a racehorse, the racing Greyhound has developed physical attributes so that he can run at top speed. For example, the Greyhound has a larger heart than any other breed of dog; in fact, it is comparable in size to a human heart. The Greyhound's heart not only has the ability to pump blood into the working muscles at a higher level than any other dog, but it can also deliver blood at a faster rate than a human athlete's heart in a comparable sprint race. In terms of pure speed, a Greyhound can reach a top speed of approximately 42 miles per hour (67 kmph), which is slightly slower than a racehorse. The human athlete can reach a top speed of around 26 miles per hour (41 kmph).

This concentration on developing speed has had an impact on the general appearance of the track Greyhound compared to his coursing cousin. The track Greyhound is smaller in size and is slighter in build. The average height at the shoulders is 27.5 inches (70 cm) for a bitch and 29 inches (74 cm) for a dog. The weight varies between 57 lb (26 kg) and 79 lb (36 kg). The track Greyhound is more streamlined, and one of the great charms of a dog that is bred for his sporting ability alone is the diversity of types, colors, and markings that emerge. Greyhounds are always smooth-coated, but they can be black, white, brindle, fawn, and blue, or white broken with any of these colors. When racing, the Greyhound's ears will lie flat against his head, but at other times they may be carried fully erect or semi-erect. Generally speaking, it does not matter what a dog looks like, as long as he can perform on the track.

THE SHOW GREYHOUND

In the world of showing purebred (pedigree) dogs, each breed is judged against a written blueprint, known as a Breed Standard. The aim of a breeder is to produce dogs that conform as closely as possible to the stipulations of the Standard.

The show Greyhound is built on the lines of its coursing cousin.

In the early days of showing, the coursing fraternity exhibited their dogs, but they soon became disillusioned with their dogs being judged purely on appearance rather than on their performance in the field. There was a split between those who bred for the show ring and those who bred for sporting ability, and, inevitably, a difference in type emerged.

The show Greyhound probably bears a stronger resemblance to coursing dogs than to track racers, but tends to be bigger, with a longer muzzle, a narrower head, and a long, muscular neck. The chest is deeper, and the body is built in more generous proportions. The show Greyhound is a most elegant dog, but it would be unlikely to stand the test of speed or stamina on a racetrack.

THE COMPANION GREYHOUND

It seems incredible that the racing Greyhound, a finely tuned athlete, can adapt to life as a family companion. To those who do not know the breed, there are fears that a retired Greyhound will need huge amounts of exercise. Many are concerned that a dog that has been bred to chase will be a menace in a domestic situation. And there are those who believe that a dog who has lived all his life in a racing kennel will not be able to adapt to a home environment.

Obviously, some dogs find it harder than others to make the transition from racer to companion, but, in the vast majority of cases, the retired Greyhound becomes an ideal pet. In the Breed Standard, the Greyhound's temperament is described as "intelligent, gentle, affectionate and even-tempered" – but even this glowing report hardly does the breed justice. The Greyhound has a superb temperament: he is kind, gentle, and loving, yet he is not too demanding. Most Greyhounds also get on well with children.

Chasing is part of a Greyhound's nature, and specialized breeding has obviously developed this aspect of the breed's temperament. It is true that the instinct to chase never truly dies, so most Greyhound owners keep their dogs on a lead in public places rather than take a chance with them. However, there are a number of Greyhounds that do not show such a strong chasing instinct. This is often termed as having a lower "prey-drive," and Greyhounds of this type have learned to live in harmony with other dogs, and sometimes even with cats.

In the majority of cases of Greyhounds rehomed from racing kennels, the adaptation to domestic life is relatively straightforward. Racing kennels generally have a strict regime of feeding, exercise, grooming and rest periods, and, as a result, most retired Greyhounds thrive on a routine existence.

Perhaps most interesting of all, the Greyhound – universally acknowledged as the athlete of the canine world – is, at heart, a couch potato! Greyhounds love their creature comforts, and a warm, comfortable bed – preferably on the sofa – is their heart's desire. A Greyhound will undoubtedly enjoy the exercise he is given, but his requirements are modest – and he will be just as keen as you to return home to the fireside on a cold night!

The gentle Greyhound makes a wonderful companion.

CHAPTER TWO

UNDERSTANDING RACING DOGS

Many people who decide to adopt a retired Greyhound have absolutely no interest in racing. They may never have attended a race meeting or placed a bet on a dog. This does not mean that they are not well qualified to own a retired Greyhound, but in order to understand how the ex-racer's mind works, it helps to know something about his former life. Obviously, every country has its own way of doing things, but the cycle of breeding, rearing, and racing is broadly the same in Ireland, Britain, the United States, and Australia – the nations that are most closely involved with the sport.

BREEDING A RACING GREYHOUND

In the world of Greyhound racing, as little as possible is left to chance. If a dog is to be successful on the track, it must be bred for the job. Before a mating ever takes place, extensive research goes into planning the litter. The bitch will probably have finished her racing career, but it is not just her results on the track that will be taken into account. Her pedigree will be closely studied to discover not only who her parents are, but how her grandparents and great-grandparents performed on the track, and whether they were successful in passing on their racing ability.

The bitch's pedigree must then be matched with a suitable sire. In most cases, this will be a dog who is advertised at stud following a top-ranking racing career. However, some stud dogs are sought after for their prestigious bloodlines alone, regardless of whether they have achieved anything spectacular in racing terms. The pedigree of the stud dog must complement the bitch's lines, and, in most cases, it is best to avoid dogs that are too closely related. The breeder will be looking at the bloodlines for the most significant characteristics, such as chasing instinct, sprinting ability, and stamina, as well as the incidence of any inherited conditions, before making a decision.

Although the owner of a retired Greyhound is not concerned with bloodlines, the intensive research that goes into breeding is of great benefit. The incidence of inherited disorders in racing Greyhounds is very low, and soundness of temperament is outstanding.

The Birth of a Litter

After all the planning, assuming everything has gone according to plan, the litter will be born approximately 63 days after the dog and bitch have been mated. Some bitches have their puppies in a home environment; some of the owner-trainers may keep just a couple of Greyhounds who are very much a part of the family. But most Greyhounds whelp in kennels with specially designed facilities. In some of the bigger establishments, a number of brood bitches will be kenneled in the same block, each in her own whelping pen.

The average size of litter is between six and eight puppies, and Greyhounds usually adapt well to motherhood. Maiden bitches – those whelping for the first time – may need a little guidance, but the established brood bitches know the score. For the first few weeks, they will cater for all their puppies' needs, feeding and cleaning them. The breeder's job is to keep the bitch well supplied with top-quality food and fluids. The demands of feeding a litter are very strenuous, and the bitch must be fed well to encourage her to produce sufficient milk.

By three weeks, the puppies will be up on their feet. Their eyes will be open, and their sense of hearing will be developing. The puppies will start eating solid food, first cereal and then meat meals. They are usually fed from a communal dish to encourage rivalry between the littermates. However, if a pup is not getting his share, he will be fed separately.

The pups are completely weaned by six weeks, but they will generally stay with their mother

At five weeks of age, these Greyhound puppies are well on their way to being weaned.

Youngsters enjoy the freedom to run and exercise themselves while they are growing.

until they are eight weeks old.

Some puppies are sold by the time they are 12 weeks of age. By this time, they will be registered with the national racing authority, and they will have an ear tattoo bearing their own personal identity number. Many litters are not broken up, and the puppies or "saplings" will be reared together until they are ready for racing.

Rearing

Rearing is a vital part of a racing Greyhound's life. A dog's success on the track will depend on his growth and development, and so feeding and exercise are top priorities.

Breeders vary in their methods of rearing, and, obviously, it also depends on the facilities that are available. Mary Butler, one of the top breeders in the United States, has an 80-acre farm in Abilene, Kansas. She rears up to 30 litters a year, accommodating the youngsters in a series of pens that have indoor and outdoor facilities.

The Greyhounds are allowed the freedom to exercise as much as they want, building up their muscles and improving their balance and co-ordination. The chasing instinct is encouraged by giving them empty plastic bottles and other toys to play with.

Mary feeds her puppies a mixture of cooked meat and dry food three times a day until they are four months old. She also provides dry food on a free-choice basis so that the puppies can get extra food in the runs if they are hungry. At four months of age, the pups move on to raw meat and dry biscuit and are fed once a day.

Ireland has long been acknowledged as a great producer of racing Greyhounds, and an open rearing method is still preferred there. Sean and Michael Dunphy have a worldwide reputation as breeders of top-quality Greyhounds, and they rear 50 to 60 pups a year on their family farm in Portlaw, County Waterford.

The land is split into two parts, and a pack of Greyhounds, roughly similar in age, will be reared in each part. The youngsters are allowed total freedom to run wherever they want, and playtime is unlimited. Sometimes, there is the odd mishap if a Greyhound plays too roughly or misses his footing, but the aim is to rear tough, fit animals – and they obviously thrive on it. The dogs are also allowed to meet visitors who come to the house so that they are confident with people.

The Dunphys' dogs are fed three times a day until they are seven months old. This meal is usually a meat-and-biscuit mixture. They then move on to a diet of cereal for breakfast and a main meal of biscuit and raw meat.

Schooling

Greyhounds enjoy a remarkably untroubled puppyhood, but the time comes when they must get down to the serious job of schooling. Again, the age this starts varies from breeder to breeder. Most will accustom a dog to a collar and lead from around eight months, and, before they are 12 months old, most youngsters will have had a couple of trial runs behind a drag lure. This helps the breeder to evaluate their chasing ability, and the dog learns to balance himself going around bends.

When serious schooling gets underway, the Greyhounds must leave the freedom of the paddocks and come into kennels. They are still given the opportunity for free-running and play, but they must learn to accept a more formal environment. In the United States, Greyhounds are usually housed in individual crates, and so the youngsters must get used to this new form of accommodation. In the UK, Greyhounds are usually kenneled in pairs; a mix of male and female generally works best.

Before a Greyhound starts running against other dogs, he must wear a muzzle. This is a simple piece of equipment made of wire or plastic, and Greyhounds rarely object to them. They often recognize the muzzle as a prelude to a race, and so they become as excited as a pet dog when seeing his lead.

To begin with, Greyhounds are hand-slipped

A racing kennel in the United States, where the dogs are housed in crates.

(released by hand), when they get to the track, but the next step is to go into the starting traps. Most breeders start with just one trap, and the dog is walked into and straight out of the trap. He then goes into the trap with the exit gate open. The lure is started, and the Greyhound sets out. When the dog is confident with this procedure, he will be put in the trap with the exit closed, and the gate is sprung open as soon as the lure is within the Greyhound's vision.

Once a Greyhound has got the idea of coming out of the traps and chasing the lure, he will then be tried alongside other dogs. This can be a decisive moment, as some Greyhounds become more interested in running with the other dogs than chasing the lure. At this stage, the dog's times will be recorded. This will give an indication of the dog's early pace – how fast he gets to the bend – and his final time for the distance covered.

Hurdle racing is a test of both speed and athleticism.

Hurdle racing is a popular variation on racing on the flat, although it is has not been adopted in the United States. In fact, few Greyhounds are schooled to jump over hurdles at the beginning of their careers. A trainer may try a dog over hurdles if he lacks true sprinting ability, or if his instinct to chase is not as keen as the trainer would like. The added interest of clearing hurdles can sharpen a dog up – and it is certainly a wonderful sight to watch a hurdler in action.

Most Greyhounds will take to hurdles naturally. They are started on an easy obstacle, such as a straw bale, to give them confidence, and then they are tried with the lure. The hurdles on the track are topped with brush so they are inviting to jump.

RACING CAREER

Greyhounds may change hands a number of times during their racing careers depending on their performance. Dogs are often bought after they have competed in their first couple of official races. At this stage, they are chasing the lure, and they have some race times to be judged by. They will then start racing at a track, hopefully working their way up from the lowest grade.

The fastest hounds may then compete in open races against the top dogs at other tracks. The swiftest Greyhounds can be entered in prestigious national races, competing with other dogs at higher levels until the finals are run. Prize money is awarded at all levels, with open race winners earning bigger cash prizes. Finals races are even more valuable as they are often sponsored.

Kennel Life

In most cases, a Greyhound will be bought for racing and will then be placed with a trainer, ready to start his career. Depending on the size of the establishment, the trainer will be assisted

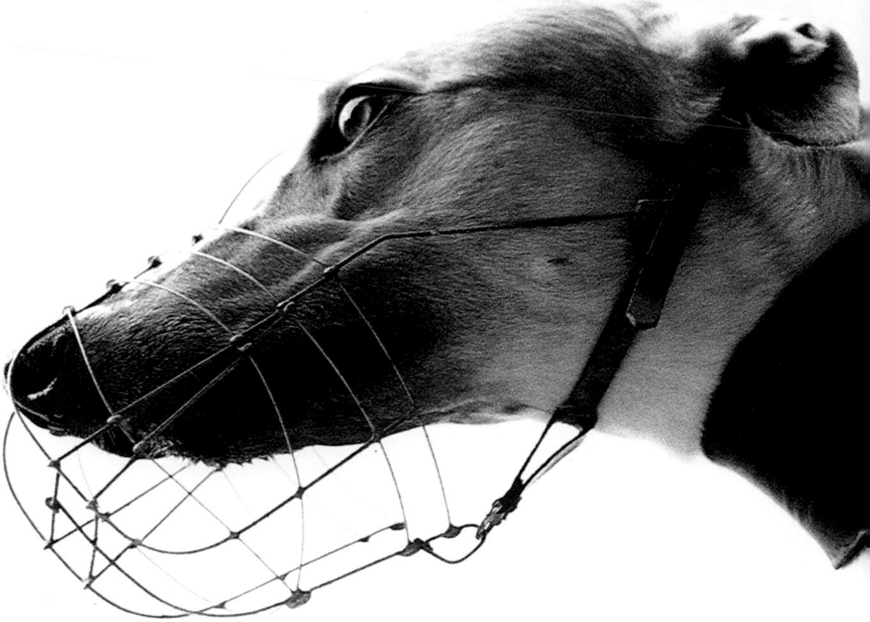

Routine is all-important in a well-run kennel.

by a number of kennel staff. Each member of the staff may be responsible for an allocated number of Greyhounds. This means that the Greyhound will get used to the person who feeds, grooms, and exercises him, and, when he goes to the track, he will be walked around and taken to the traps by the same person. A number of owner-trainers keep just a few Greyhounds. Their dogs may be kept in kennels, or they may live in the house; they tend to be better socialized than Greyhounds kept in big racing kennels.

Routine is essential when keeping a large number of animals, and a well-regulated kennel will help to produce fit, healthy dogs that are happy and relaxed at home and ready to respond to the demands of racing when they get to the track.

Feeding

Feeding is a very important aspect of keeping racing dogs, and every trainer keeps a close check on how his dogs are responding to their diet. This varies depending on the methods of the individual trainer, but most will feed a cereal-type breakfast, and the main meal will be biscuit and meat, which may be either raw or cooked. Some trainers also use complete food, and others may provide rice or pasta to supplement carbohydrate levels. Fish or chicken may be fed as a change from red meat. The weight of each Greyhound is closely monitored, and trainers will discover each dog's ideal racing weight. The dogs will be weighed regularly to ensure they do not go too far over, or under, the desired weight.

Greyhounds are treated like athletes, and grooming and massage is part of their daily ritual. Each dog will be brushed and combed thoroughly; their teeth will be cleaned, and their nails will be trimmed when necessary. Massage is an important part of caring for a racing dog. A liniment of oil is worked into the body, gently massaging all the muscles. This process helps to improve muscle tone and circulation.

Lead-walking is a beneficial form of exercise for racing Greyhounds – and it can become a family affair!

Exercise

Exercise is the key to producing a fit dog, but this does not necessarily mean testing a dog at racing speed. Many trainers see great benefits in walking as a means of strengthening tendons, ligaments, and toes and promoting steady breathing. A pair of Greyhounds are often lead-walked together, probably for two 15-minute sessions each day. They are usually walked on a hard surface. Most Greyhounds also exercise in grass paddocks, and there may be the opportunity to release Greyhounds on specially made gallops as part of their fitness program.

Some trainers favor the use of a walking machine. This is driven by a motor; the dog is exercised on a type of conveyor belt and is held in position by a bar across the front of the machine. Generally, two Greyhounds can be exercised at a time, but they must always be supervised. In Australia, some of the bigger kennels use a rotating walker which can accommodate as many as 12 Greyhounds at a time. The positive aspect of a walking machine is that it can be used in all types of weather. It reduces labor, but the Greyhound does not receive comparable benefits from such nonpersonal exercise. Mechanical exercise is boring for the dog; it offers no change of scenery and no interaction with the handler.

In the United States, walking is not so highly rated as a means of exercise. A trainer is more likely to turn out a group of Greyhounds (either all males or all females) in a paddock, and allow them to exercise under close supervision. The dogs are muzzled to prevent injury.

Swimming is also used as a form of exercise. It is particularly useful when bringing Greyhounds back to racing fitness after a layoff caused by injury. It provides valuable exercise without putting strain on toes, tendons, and ligaments. Some of the bigger racing kennels have their own purpose-built pools. These are usually circular in shape with a central platform. A long rod is attached to the Greyhound's collar so that he can be guided around the pool. In most cases, Greyhounds soon get used to

In sprint races, the getaway from the traps is often decisive.

this routine, and many seem to enjoy the experience.

Responsibilities

The owners of racing Greyhounds are not always seen in the most favorable light. The popular perception is that they are only interested in betting on their dogs and picking up the prize money. While the majority of owners prefer to keep their relationship on a business footing – paying for the Greyhound's upkeep and ensuring that he is receiving the best care and training – there are others who get more involved. At the weekend, many racing kennels allow owners to come and see their Greyhounds and to take them for a walk on the grounds. Both dog and owner derive a great deal of pleasure from the relationship.

Race-day Routine

Greyhounds usually race once or twice a week. Although each race may last no longer than 30 seconds, the demands on the body are huge. It is vital not to overexert a dog or he will become jaded and will not give his best. Many Greyhounds are given rest periods from the track; with bitches, this will usually coincide with their seasonal cycle.

On race days, the aim is to keep the Greyhound as quiet and relaxed as possible so that he conserves his energy for the task ahead. Assuming that the race meeting is in the evening, breakfast will usually be fed as normal. Then, in the early afternoon, the Greyhounds will be fed a small meal. Exercise will be confined to a short walk, or a limited period in the paddock.

The Greyhounds are muzzled and transported to the track in a van or truck that is fitted out with crates. A Greyhound that is kept by a small owner-trainer will probably travel in a car.

At the track, the Greyhounds must be kenneled for a set period of time prior to racing. Security is in force to prevent any outside interference with the dogs. In the UK, random urine samples are taken before racing to test for drugs. In the United States, two dogs from each race are drug-tested after racing. Each

A Greyhound's racing career is relatively short-lived.

Greyhound is weighed and his ear-marks are checked. Prior to the race, the Greyhound is taken from the kennel. His lightweight racing muzzle will be fitted, and he will wear a racing jacket, showing the color and number of his trap draw. In the UK, six dogs compete in a race; the United States generally has eight-dog races.

While bets are being placed on the race, the Greyhounds are paraded around the track. This gives the dogs a chance to warm up after lying in the kennel. Some handlers will give their dogs a quick massage at this stage.

The dogs are then put into the traps, their collars and leads are removed, and the handlers leave the track. At the sound of the lure, the dogs usually start barking and crouch down in readiness for the traps to open. As the lure comes into view, the traps are sprung open and the dogs shoot out.

In sprint races, it is often the dog's starting (trapping) ability, and his speed to the first bend that are decisive. In longer races, which may cover six or even eight bends, staying ability will come into play. As the dogs near the finishing line, the sound of the crowd reaches a crescendo as punters shout their dogs home. The time is clocked as the first dog crosses the line, and the distances between each of the dogs is recorded. A dummy lure is sprung, and the Greyhounds are caught by their handlers.

Panting heavily and often covered with sand from the track surface, the Greyhounds are led back to the racing kennels. Each Greyhound has his feet checked and is washed down to get rid of the sand; sand is also cleared from around the eyes and nose. When his breathing has returned to normal, the dog will be given a drink of water.

At the end of the meeting, the Greyhounds are transported home. Back at the kennels, they are given their main meal of the day and then allowed to settle for the night.

A retired Greyhound can offer many years of companionship.

RACING INJURIES

Greyhounds love to race, and there is absolutely no hardship involved in allowing a dog to pursue his natural instinct. Most racing Greyhounds are given the finest possible care, and the kennel regime of feeding, grooming, massage, exercise, and racing provides a varied and stimulating environment.

Greyhounds generally have a far more interesting life than other dogs that live controlled, kennel lives.

The downside of racing is the injuries that can be sustained. If a number of dogs are racing at speed around a circular track, it is inevitable that they will knock into each other. This may be little more than a bump, or it may cause a dog to lose his footing, resulting in a serious injury, such as a broken wrist or hock. The stress of racing can put serious strain on toes, tendons, and ligaments, and injury may result.

In many cases, the injury can be treated. Modern techniques, such as magnetic therapy and ultrasound, are used with great success. A fracture is obviously a far more serious problem, and while some Greyhounds have returned to racing after surgery, for most it signals the end of their careers.

RETIREMENT

The Greyhound has a short racing life. Most

will start racing at around 15 months and will retire at three to four years of age. Short-race speedsters, called sprinters, usually retire younger than long-distance endurance racers. Distance dogs often retire by the time they are four or five years of age, although a number may race for longer. Some Greyhounds may take up marathon racing, where early speed is not so important. If a dog has suffered an injury that has impaired his racing ability, he will be retired early.

In some cases, a Greyhound may need rehoming because he is not good enough to race: he may not have the instinct to chase, he may be too slow, or he may be a "fighter," which simply means that he is more intent on nudging and running alongside his fellow Greyhounds rather than chasing the lure. These dogs will tend to be younger than the average retired racer.

If a male Greyhound has been highly successful on the track, he may be used at stud, and a whole new career opens up. A bitch, with good bloodlines and racing ability, may well be used for breeding. However, for the vast majority of retired racers, the future is uncertain. The average life expectancy of a Greyhound is between 12 and 15 years, so there are many years ahead.

Thankfully, the racing authorities are increasingly aware of the need to rehome retired Greyhounds, and adoption agencies and their staff work tirelessly to find suitable homes. There are some owners of racing Greyhounds who will take a dog into their own home on retirement, but these are very much in the minority. However, Greyhounds must still be maintained, whether they are racing or not, and a far greater percentage of owners are taking on this responsibility until new homes can be found.

The success rate of rehoming retired Greyhounds is increasing. In the United States, approximately 16,000 former racers are adopted each year. In the UK, the total is around 2,000.

For those who make the decision to adopt a racing Greyhound, the rewards are tremendous. The King of Sighthounds may not be showing off his racing skills to the world any more, but, if anything, the ex-racer makes an even bigger success of his second career – as a beautiful and loving companion.

CHAPTER THREE

ADOPTING A GREYHOUND

Taking on a dog is a major commitment, regardless of the animal's breed, age, or background. It should be a decision that is made in the cold light of day and not in a rush of sentiment. Once a dog has become part of the family, you must be responsible for all his needs for the rest of his days. Hopefully, this will be the start of a great new relationship – but take your time before making up your mind!

THE PROS

There are many positive aspects of taking on a retired Greyhound.

- You will not have to cope with the demands of a puppy.
- You can see exactly what you are getting in terms of both temperament and appearance.
- Careful breeding means that racing Greyhounds have a very low incidence of inherited disorders. Temperament is universally sound in the breed.
- During their racing lives, most Greyhounds will have had the best of care in terms of diet, exercise, and veterinary attention.
- Exercise and grooming requirements are moderate.

THE CONS

There are always two sides to an argument, and so you should take possible negatives into account.

- You will miss out on the puppy phase of owning a dog.
- Racing Greyhounds are used to living in kennels, and you will have to re-educate your dog to living in a house.
- A racing Greyhound's experience of the outside world is limited, so he will need a program of socialization.
- The instinct to chase is present in all Greyhounds.

GREAT EXPECTATIONS

When weighing the pros and cons of owning a Greyhound, you should also examine your own expectations so that you are confident that this is the right breed for you.

A Greyhound is beautiful to look at, and you will certainly enjoy having such an elegant creature in your home. Loving, yet undemanding, a Greyhound's companionship is something to be greatly valued.

In terms of trainability, Greyhounds (in common with other members of the hound family) are not the most responsive of dogs. However, it is relatively easy to teach basic commands, and to train your dog to be generally well behaved (see Chapter 6).

Consider your lifestyle, and work out if you have the time to commit to a new member of the family before deciding on adopting a Greyhound.

Most Greyhounds soon adapt to living in a family.

LIFESTYLES

It is fortunate that Greyhounds are an adaptable breed. Not only can they make the transition from racing dog to companion, but they can also fit in with a number of different lifestyles.

However, it is important that you consider the specific needs of the Greyhound so that you can be confident that you are providing a suitable home.

The Family Dog

A Greyhound's calm, placid outlook on life makes him an ideal choice of family dog. Most Greyhounds enjoy the companionship of older children and like to be involved with the comings and goings of family life. However, this may not be the case with a family that has very small children of toddler age and below. Children of this age are often on all fours and can be unpredictable in their actions. A Greyhound, who has not been brought up with children, may find this hard to cope with, or even frightening.

Working Partnership

If you have a part-time job, a retired Greyhound may well be a good choice – as long as you do not have to leave your dog for too long. Racing dogs are used to being kenneled, and so they understand the routine of settling down quietly, without human companionship.

However, it is important not to leave your Greyhound the moment he arrives in his new home. He will need to be eased into the separation so that he does not feel as though he is being abandoned. Once a dog has settled, he will be quite happy to be left for a period not exceeding four hours. In the time that you spend at home, your Greyhound should be given plenty of attention and companionship so that you can build up a good relationship.

Female Greyhounds are often preferred as prospective adoptees, but males make equally good pets.

Never Too Old

Older people are often deterred from taking on a dog because they fear they will not be able to cope with the antics of a lively puppy. A retired Greyhound, who likes nothing better than lounging on the sofa and will walk calmly on the lead, is an excellent choice for those who want to enjoy dog ownership at a more gentle pace.

REHOMING PROSPECTS

The length of time it takes to rehome a Greyhound varies enormously. It may be as little as two weeks, or it could take as long as six months. The younger dogs are the first to go. The older the dog, the more difficult it is to rehome. Prospective owners are obviously keen to have a dog that has been retired because he does not chase the lure, or has a very low prey-drive. Most prefer a Greyhound that has suffered no serious injuries – even though the dog has been treated and is perfectly sound.

Generally, bitches are easier to rehome, probably because most prospective owners think they will be smaller and less dominant. Pat Bannister, who runs the rehoming scheme for Wimbledon Stadium, Britain's premier racetrack, says: "It is a mystery to us why people prefer bitches. The males are often more easy-going and laid-back. The bitches tend to be a bit more bouncy and full of themselves. But I think people are often attracted by the smaller size, and they think a bitch will be less trouble."

HOME AND AWAY

Jack and Rose Marie Stoeffler, who live in New Cumberland, Pennsylvania, adopted two Greyhounds while they were both still working. Then, when they retired, they took to the road, traveling across the United States in a motor home with their two dogs on board.

"We first read about racing Greyhounds in a magazine article, and then we saw a program on television," said Jack. "Both Rose Marie and I were deeply concerned about the fate of Greyhounds when they were no longer winning races, and we decided that we would like to go ahead and adopt.

"In 1990, we sent off our application to the dog shelter, and we were able to state the sex, color, and age of the Greyhound we would like to adopt. We wanted a fawn female, between two and three years old. We were allocated Dorie, a silver-fawn female, aged two and a half years – so we got exactly what we wanted.

"We learned that Dorie had broken her leg when racing, and, although she had made a good recovery, she was no longer in the winners' circle. Her owner and trainer were both determined to have her rehomed rather than have her put down.

"When Dorie first arrived home with us she was a bit groggy as she had been spayed only the day before. We were in such a hurry to get her, we didn't even have time to buy a crate for her. So we said: 'The whole house can be her crate' – and it worked out just fine. She had only two accidents before she was completely clean in the house.

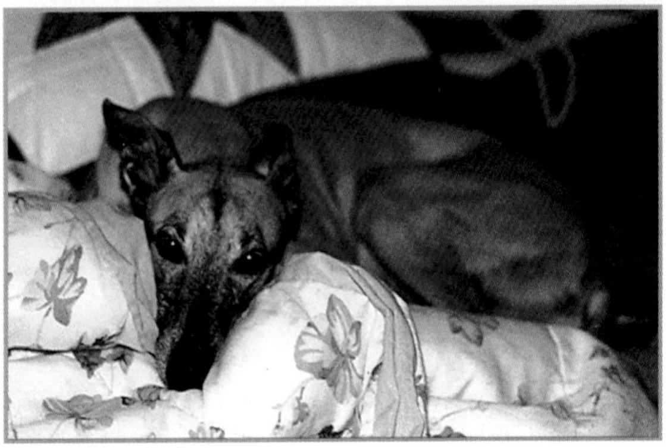

As Dorie became more confident, her personality began to emerge.

"At that time, we were both working, so Dorie had to spend some time on her own. I used to come back at lunch-time to let her out and give her some TLC, and, as Rose Marie was a teacher, she was home by mid-afternoon.

"We did not have a problem keeping a dog in this situation. Greyhounds do not need a lot of exercise – a walk from the sofa to the refrigerator suits them fine! In fact, we took Dorie out three or four times a day, and always included her in trips out in the car so she was part of the family activities.

"Right from the beginning, Dorie was a very sweet little girl, but she didn't know how to play. It took her a year to work out what to do with dog toys. As she became more confident, her personality started to come out. There was one time when Rose Marie left three pounds of ground meat defrosting in the sink – and Dorie ate the lot!"

HOME FOR KEEPS

In 1993, Jack and Rose Marie adopted their second Greyhound, a black female called Pandy.

"Pandy had already been placed in a home, but the new owners informed the adoption agency that she was very withdrawn," said Jack. "The veterinarian checked her over, and he said she was going downhill emotionally. The adoption agency asked if we would foster her, so I drove for two and a half hours to collect her. I put her in the back of the car and drove home. I rang the agency and said: 'We can't foster this dog – we're keeping her!'

"Pandy was afraid of everything. To begin with, she went to the furthest corner of the house and just lay there. She wouldn't even get up for her food.

Pandy and Dorie enjoying life on the road.

"We were advised to work with her on the lead, as Greyhounds are used to this, and gradually we got her to follow us around the house. It took a long time to gain her trust – it was a year before she accepted all the family members. Now she sticks so close to us, we call her our Velcro Dog."

In 1995 Rose Marie retired, followed a year later by Jack. Rose Marie had to undergo major surgery, and, although she made a good recovery, they decided to reassess their lives.

"We bought a 28-ft motor home and decided to travel and see our beautiful country," said Jack. "The two dogs came with us and they soon adapted to life on the road. Their chief concern was who got the best bed! While we enjoyed seeing all the new sights, Dorie and Pandy enjoyed sniffing all the new smells."

Sadly, Dorie died aged nine, suffering from intestinal problems. "It was a terrible shock for us because it all happened so quickly," said Jack. "Pandy missed her a little, but she is so attached to us that she just got on with her own life. She has now traveled over 30,000 miles with us."

Now Jack and Rose Marie have even more ambitious plans. They are selling their house to buy a larger motor home, and they are going to become full-time travelers. Needless to say, Pandy is coming too...

In the United States, most prospective owners also prefer females. Cynthia Branigan, who runs Make Peace With Animals in Pennsylvania, says: "Many people have the misconception that females are more affectionate. Size can also be an issue, but I point out that we have placed 75-lb females and 62-lb males! In the end, we place more males than females; but there is no question that females are preferred initially.

"Color can also be a cause for concern. I have noticed that a fair number of people remark that they will adopt any color except black – it seems that many people find black dogs frightening!"

FIRST CONTACT

There are many different types of people who want to adopt a Greyhound. They may be rich or poor, status seekers or humanitarians, experienced dog owners or first-timers, and there are those who just want the dog that is most in need – no matter the appearance or age. The adoption agencies must try to sort out these potential owners and find out who can genuinely provide a suitable home. They must then try to match characters and lifestyles and find a Greyhound who is most likely to fit in with a given set of circumstances.

In the UK, where geography is less of a problem, potential owners are encouraged to visit the kennels to see the Greyhounds that need rehoming. Some may never have had contact with the breed before, so it is important that they start off by seeing lots of different

Greyhounds and getting used to the breed. Potential owners are encouraged to visit the kennels on a number of occasions and to take a number of different Greyhounds out for a walk on the grounds.

In the United States, it is often more difficult to make the trip to visit a rehoming kennel, and so a lot of initial work is done by letter and by phone. Following an application, the adoption agency will send out an information package, outlining all the pros and cons of owning a Greyhound and detailing the care that is involved. They will ask for personal details in order to build up a profile of the applicant. Questions include:

- Do you go out to work? If so, for how long?
- Are there children in the family? What are their ages?
- Do you own a cat or any other small animal?
- Do you own a dog?
- Is your yard securely fenced?
- Have you had experience owning dogs?

The adoption agency will then check out references and follow this up with a phone call to find out as much as possible about the individual circumstances of the applicant.

ADOPTION AGENCIES

Now that you have decided to take on a retired Greyhound, how do you go about adopting one?

In the United States, there is a directory of Greyhound Adoption organizations. Some advertise on the Internet, but information can also be obtained from the National Greyhound Association, which represents racing tracks in the United States.

In the UK, the Retired Greyhound Trust co-ordinates the rehoming of retired dogs from tracks that are licensed by the National Greyhound Racing Club. A number of other voluntary organizations find homes for retired Greyhounds, including those that have run on independent, unlicensed tracks.

In Europe, Spain is the only country where professional Greyhound racing takes place. Unfortunately, the care of racing dogs in Spain has often fallen below an acceptable standard, and the problem has become acute when dogs are no longer fit for racing. This situation has attracted a lot of adverse publicity, and voluntary groups are campaigning to try to improve the welfare of Spanish Greyhounds. Groups in Belgium, Switzerland, Germany, and the UK are also hard at work finding homes for retired Spanish racers.

THE ADOPTION PROCESS

All adoption agencies have their own methods of rehoming Greyhounds. These may vary in detail, but the general principles are the same. The top priority is the future well-being of every Greyhound that is adopted, and the chief task is to find the best match of dog and owner.

Depending on the agency, Greyhounds who are put up for adoption will remain in racing kennels, or they may be in kennels run by the rehoming organization. If a dog has been running at a licensed track, he will have a racing book that will contain a complete record of his racing career. This record will include details of the sire and dam, date of birth, and a personal identification, noting color and markings, as well as ear tattoos. Every official trial and race will be recorded, with details of the dog's individual performance. Many potential owners find this record of great interest, and, if a Greyhound has changed hands several times, it may be the only complete record of the dog's history.

On the other side of the coin, large numbers of Greyhounds arrive at rehoming kennels with no paperwork. In some cases, nothing is known about a dog; in other instances, the bare minimum of name, age, and color has been supplied.

When a Greyhound is put up for adoption, the rehoming staff will make a thorough assessment of each dog. If the trainer is known, this can be useful as he or she will know of any particular behavioral traits and will have information concerning any racing injuries the dog sustained. The rehoming staff take the dogs out, as well as feeding them and grooming them. This interaction helps to build up a picture of each Greyhound that will be invaluable when it comes to finding a suitable home.

Some adoption agencies undertake basic training and socialization to prepare the Greyhounds for their new lives as companions. Where possible, a cat is kept on the premises, and the Greyhounds, who are obviously on leads and muzzled, can be tested to see if they are cat-keen or not.

During their stays in kennels, Greyhounds may be neutered. Some agencies have a set policy of neutering both males and females prior to rehoming. Others neuter bitches, but only neuter males if there is an indication of aggression, or any other behavior trait, that may cause a problem. Some agencies leave neutering to the discretion of the new owners.

Each Greyhound's character is assessed before going forward for adoption.

Try to find out as much as possible about Greyhounds before making the decision to adopt.

The Home Visit

If at all possible, the adoption procedure should involve a home visit, when one of the rehoming staff will go to the potential owner's home to meet the family and check out the environment.

The garden is usually the chief area of concern. Greyhounds are not usually great escape artists, but, if a dog suddenly catches sight of something – such as the neighbor's cat or a squirrel – there will be no stopping him. The garden should be securely fenced to a height of 5 ft. (1.52 m) minimum, but ideally to 6 ft. (1.83 m). At least the lower 4 ft. (1.22 m) should be solid. This means that the Greyhound cannot see what is going on next door and so temptations are avoided.

The home-checker tries to meet all the family and will discuss the specific needs of a Greyhound with them.

"After a while, you get a gut feeling as to whether a family is suitable," said Pat Bannister. "It's the people who ask lots of questions and listen to the advice that are most likely to be suitable owners."

Cynthia Branigan backs this up 100 percent. "We tell adopters that the only dumb questions are the ones they don't ask!

"The more we know about an applicant, the more chance we have of making a successful match. By talking to people, especially in their own home, you can find out what their attitude is towards dogs, and you can see how they treat their own pets, if they have any. For example, there are some people who think it is quite acceptable to tie up a dog all day, or they may not bother with vaccination programs. Obviously, these people would not be allowed to adopt.

"If we are going into a family, we also like to see how the children behave. Without exception, all adopters claim their children are angels – some are, some aren't!"

The home-checker will discuss working arrangements, to ensure that the Greyhound is not to be left for too long a period, as well as giving information on feeding, exercise, and settling-in procedures.

Matchmaking

Once an application is approved, it is a matter of finding the most suitable Greyhound. Like all animals, Greyhounds are individuals. The breed may share certain traits, but each dog will have his own personality.

For example, some Greyhounds will be more lively and outgoing, while others are more docile. Some will walk quietly on the lead, others will try to pull ahead. One Greyhound may thrive in a lively family environment; another dog, who is more timid, would be better suited to a quieter home. There are Greyhounds who have a very high prey-drive and will chase everything in sight. There are others who can be classed as "nonchasers," who have a very low prey-drive and will be far more likely to get on with other animals.

The adoption agency compares the profile of the applicant with the dogs that need rehoming and makes a recommendation. If the applicant has visited a kennel, they may well have a preference for a particular Greyhound. This is taken into consideration, assuming that the rehoming staff think they are making a sensible choice.

Cynthia Branigan started off by allowing adopters to make their own choice, but then she decided on a change of policy.

"I realized that we knew more about the dogs than the prospective adopter, and we really knew more about what kind of dog the potential owners should have. Many people are taken in by a pretty face or a sad story, but this may not be the best companion for them overall. However, there are always exceptions, and I know of many successful cases where the adopter has been allowed to choose."

Cynthia's organization, in common with a number of other adoption agencies in the United States, uses a system of fostering. A Greyhound is placed in a foster home to see how he reacts to a domestic setting. For example, if a dog is to be placed in a home with children, he will be fostered with a family that has a similar setup. If the new owners are going to be out at work, the Greyhound will be tested with someone who is also working to see how he reacts to being left. A dog will be cat-tested twice before he is placed in a home that has a cat.

"The only situation we cannot duplicate is how a dog will react without any animal companions, as all our foster families have other pets," said Cynthia.

There is an art to matching the Greyhound with his new owner.

FOSTERING TRUST

Lorraine Farrell has been helping to rehome racing Greyhounds for the last ten years. She heard about the plight of ex-racers and adopted her first Greyhound, Delbert, in 1991. She now has five Greyhounds living at home, and she works as a foster parent, getting ex-racers ready for their new lives as companion dogs.

"I have learned most of what I know by trial and error," said Lorraine. "I have found that generally Greyhounds are docile, quiet, gentle, and loving pets. They, like people, have individual personalities – some are more outgoing, others are more reserved or shy. I have come to believe that there are few 'bad dogs', but many 'bad owners.'

"We got Delbert when the children were very young – my daughter, Leigh, was six, and my son, Kyle, was four. Greyhounds are good with children of any age, as long as the parents are conscientious. It is important that toddlers are never left alone with animals. Yet parents often forget this warning within the first week or so after a Greyhound has arrived in a new home.

"Young children unintentionally hurt animals – a crayon in the eye, or falling on a sleeping animal when toddlers are trying to walk. A growl is a dog's warning, but it is a warning that most children do not hear. For this reason, I think it is better to place a Greyhound in a family where the youngest child is four years or above. At that age, they can be taught to respect a dog's privacy, allowing the animal to be left alone when it is eating or sleeping. They can also learn not to pull at the ears or the tail.

Lorraine Farrell's home has been a sanctuary to many former racers.

"Because I am a stay-at-home Mom, I am usually given the special-needs dogs to foster. These are Greyhounds that may be recovering from a track injury, or they may be sick, requiring medication several times a day. I also get the very shy dogs who may well have been mistreated. I teach that dog to love and trust again. These Greyhounds may be with foster parents for a few months, and then they are placed in a home where a 'special-needs' dog is requested."

GREYHOUNDS AND OTHER ANIMALS

Why do rehoming agencies have to be so careful about placing Greyhounds in a home with other animals? If you see things from the Greyhound's perspective, the problem becomes easier to understand.

Racing Greyhounds live a secluded life, and although they are generally well socialized with people, they will probably have had no contact with other animals apart from Greyhounds. Most Greyhounds will never have seen any other type of dog, let alone a cat or any other small animal. It is therefore hardly surprising that the Greyhound is confused when confronted with an animal he does not recognize. Obviously, the danger is that the Greyhound's hunting instincts are awakened, and he sees every small furry animal as something he must chase.

However, the instinct to chase varies from individual to individual. Some Greyhounds have such a low prey-drive that they never make the grade on the racing track as they have little interest in chasing the lure. Obviously, this type of dog is far more likely to live in harmony with a small animal. Other Greyhounds may have been successful on the track, but their chase instinct is not awakened by small dogs or cats. It is only by testing a dog in a controlled situation that you can find out his response.

Greyhounds with a high prey-drive should never be rehomed with other animals. In fact, these dogs will always need very careful supervision, as they will see a squirrel in the garden, the neighbor's cat, or a small dog running in the park as fair game. They can be rehomed, as long as their new owner has a secure yard and provides sufficient on-lead exercise.

Canine Companions

If an adopter already has a dog, the situation must be tested carefully before a Greyhound is selected for rehoming. This can be done in a foster home, or, in some situations, the adopters are invited to bring their own dog to the kennels. The retired Greyhounds who are the most likely to react favorably (usually the lazier, more laid-back types) are put on leads and muzzled. The pet dog is walked on a lead in front of them, and reactions are noted. Some Greyhounds show instant aggression, others are clearly worried, frightened, or suspicious. The Greyhounds who show interest, but are not too stressed, are singled out.

The next step is for the potential owners to take each of these Greyhounds out with their

Many Greyhounds will have never seen any other breed of dog.

Living in peace: Some Greyhounds have a very low prey-drive and will learn not to chase cats.

pet dog. Both dogs should be on the lead, and the Greyhound should be muzzled. An experienced member of the rehoming staff can accompany them, and, again, reactions are noted. At this stage, it is fairly easy to tell whether a Greyhound is going to accept his new canine friend. But the two dogs must be given an opportunity to play in a paddock, off the lead, before the final verdict is given. For safety's sake, the Greyhound remains muzzled. However, if this, and follow-up sessions, go without a hitch, the Greyhound can go forward for adoption.

Obviously, care must be taken when the Greyhound arrives in his new home (see pages 37 and 50), but, in the vast majority of cases, a Greyhound that has gone through this series of tests can be trusted.

Greyhounds and Cats

Many retired Greyhounds live in perfect harmony with the family cat, but this cannot be relied upon. Some adoption agencies would rather steer clear of this problem and would prefer a Greyhound to go to a cat-free home – but exceptions always disprove the rule. If a potential owner has a cat and is prepared to work at the canine-feline relationship, the outcome can be successful.

Greyhounds and Small Animals

It seems like asking for trouble to expect a retired Greyhound to live with a small animal. In fact, very small animals, such as hamsters, are not a problem if reasonable care is taken (see page 52). However, guinea pigs and rabbits are very tempting, particularly if they are kept in a run in the garden during the summer months. Pet birds are also a source of trouble, particularly as the bird will need time out of its cage on a perch.

Generally, it is better to keep a retired Greyhound in a home without small animals or birds, but if the owner is prepared to exercise great care and vigilance, and the Greyhound has a particularly placid temperament, co-existence is possible.

Seeing is believing: This is a very remarkable scenario, but some Greyhounds understand that all family pets must be tolerated.

ONE COOL CAT

Diane Beatty, who is is based in Pennsylvania, has several dogs and cats, plus her Greyhound Blitzen. She also fosters Greyhounds before they are placed in homes, and her cat, Clarence, has become the Number One cat-tester.

"When you are testing a Greyhound, it is very important not to use a frightened or nervous cat, but I swear some cats just love the job," said Diane. "My big orange, male cat, Clarence, is the premier cat pro. He saunters, he purrs, he struts, he rubs against your legs in full view of the testee, and then he dashes round the room just to see what happens. Clarence is one smart cat, and I really believe he knows he is performing for an appreciative audience.

Blitzen and Clarence: Peace at last.

"We first got his measure when we brought our Greyhound, Blitzen, home. He had been fine with the 'test cat' at the adoption agency, but we made sure he was leashed and muzzled when we introduced him to Clarence. Blitzen looked somewhat menacing, and I was sure it was all a mistake and he was going to turn out to be a killer. My husband sat on the sofa and held Blitzen between his knees, the leash held right at the collar in a death grip, ready for him to explode the second he laid eyes on the poor, unsuspecting cat.

"Clarence waltzed into the room, took one look at this huge beast and leapt on to the sofa. Before I could react, he walked up to the 'beast' and walloped him in the muzzle with his furry, little de-clawed paw. Blitzen started to tremble in terror, he whined and retreated as far as he could from this small, orange monster. My husband gave the leash some slack, and Blitzen tried to get behind him. Meanwhile, Clarence gave one huge hiss, turned his back and just walked over to the arm of the sofa where he casually began to groom himself, staring down on the poor, terrified Greyhound.

"That was Blitzen's introduction to the feline race, and he knows his place in the hierarchy. We have had up to four cats living with us, including one very old, tiny, fluffball of a Himalayan, who looked the very image of a soft toy or a lure. One of my current cats is also very old and slow. She loves to sun herself on the back of Blitzen's favorite sofa, and she often falls asleep so deeply that she loses her balance and rolls off the sofa on to a sleeping Blitzen. I worried that he would react to this rude awakening, but Blitzen learned his lesson in cat interaction very early on!

"However, although I am confident that Blitzen is perfectly reliable with my cats in the house, outside is a whole different world. I have seen him chase stray cats, rabbits, and squirrels that have come into our yard. No matter how 'cat-safe' you think your Greyhound is, he should never be allowed outdoors with a small animal unsupervised."

ONE COOL CAT ▶

ONE COOL CAT

O'Henry the Greyhound with cats Billie, Stevie, and Ignatz.

FIRST REACTION

When Diane is trying out a new Greyhound, she likes a test to last for at least five minutes to give the dog, who must be on the leash and muzzled, ample time to react. "Having said that, I think you will probably have a good guesstimate of the dog's prey-drive almost immediately," she said.

"A good reaction would be if the dog ignored the cat's antics. You have to watch very closely to be sure the dog actually saw what was going on and had no reaction. If the dog looked away from the cat, especially during the running phase, I would say that was a good first reaction. I would let the dog get a little closer to the cat to see if the closer proximity made any difference.

"If there was still no reaction, or the dog appeared a little nervous, I would think this is a cat-safe dog. If the dog sniffed at the cat or appeared slightly interested but not overly so, I would also think that was a good reaction. It is natural to show some curiosity. If the dog continues to show some interest (sniffing, tail wagging, or ears coming up) but can be easily distracted, I would consider this dog to be of medium prey-drive and probably trainable."

BAD SIGN

"A bad reaction would be a dog who is trembling with excitement or barking or whining, or who becomes very stiff, one who couldn't keep his eyes off the cat or lunged forward, a dog whose attention is extremely focused on the 'prey.' Cats seem to know when dogs are not 'friendly,' and, if the cat leaves the room and the dog continues to stare at the spot where the cat disappeared, I would take this as a very bad sign."

Diane has also supervised introductions between ex-racers and other dogs, and she has discovered that every Greyhound is a case in his own right.

"We took on a Greyhound called Jake and started by introducing him to our little white dog, Odie, who was outside in the yard," said Diane. "Odie is very small, only around 10 pounds, and the new guy, Jake, was huge, close to 100 pounds.

"We introduced them with the big guy leashed and muzzled. At first, I held little Odie in my arms. When Jake showed no interest other than a perfunctory sniff, I put her on the ground, but leashed so I could pull her to safety if necessary. Jake sniffed her again and then proceeded to completely ignore her. He explored the yard and met the other 'big' dogs with no problems at all, just the usual 'introductory' warning rumble from our alpha female, the German Shepherd."

TAKING PRECAUTIONS

"We monitored them outside for some time and then let Jake off the lead (although he was still muzzled for safety), and there was no hint of aggression or prey-drive at all – absolutely none. He romped around, and, if he encountered the little one, he would either sniff and walk away, or do a play-bow to try (unsuccessfully) to get Odie to play with him.

"We were confident that Jake would be fine

with the cats. In fact, we were so confident that we almost didn't take the appropriate precautions. One of those 'oh, he'll be fine, look how good he is with Odie.' But almost as an afterthought we did leash and muzzle him, and took him inside to cat-test him.

"We had our fearless Clarence to do the test. He was lying on a stool, sunning himself, when Jake came to meet him. Within half a second, we knew we were in trouble. Jake launched himself at Clarence with the most fearsome snarling and growling I have ever heard. Our poor, fearless kitty was in mid-air, literally flying out of the room. After months of intense training, Jake remained as high-prey-drive as ever with the cats.

"In a case like this, the Greyhound would need to be rehomed in a home without a cat, but we kept Jake as he had a terminal medical problem, and we knew he did not have many months to live. We ensured that he never came into contact with the cats at any time.

"However, he remained 100 percent trustworthy with our little dog. She was getting on in years and was always the last to finish her dinner. Jake would finish his and sneak up on her, trying to nudge his way in to 'help' her finish her dinner.

"The little one always turned and gave him the evil eye, and sometimes growled at him. Jake would literally turn and run away, usually with a chagrined look on his face. He looked as though he was saying, 'I know I shouldn't be afraid of that little dog, but she's mean.'

"Odie is smaller than the cats and fluffy, yet it always amazed me that Jake could be so gentle with her and so unbelievably vicious with the cats! It's just another lesson learned. Never assume that you can think like a dog. Equally, remember that a dog is an animal, and this must be respected in all our interactions with them, especially in regard to prey-drive."

GREYHOUNDS AND CHILDREN

Most racing dogs will never have met a child before, and this is another relationship that should be tested before rehoming. Most adoption agencies are not keen to place a Greyhound with a family that has very small children. The children are too young to respect the needs of an adult dog. For example, a child may crawl up to the Greyhound and startle him when he is asleep. A dog who has not been brought up with children could not be blamed for being frightened, or maybe even snapping.

Another danger is that small children are careless about closing doors, and there have been incidents of Greyhounds bolting from home when a door has been left ajar and the yard is not totally secure.

Relations between Greyhounds and children will need to be supervised in the early stages.

Older children, who have been taught to respect animals, are an entirely different matter. The Greyhound is gentle and loving by nature, and many have developed a very special relationship with the children in their family. (See page 41.)

Before allowing a Greyhound to go to a family home, the home-checker will need to be confident that the parents are willing to supervise their children with the dog, and that they understand what constitutes acceptable behavior. (Meeting the Family, see page 49.)

SIGNING UP

Before giving the final go-ahead, the new owners must sign a contract with the adoption agency. This stipulates certain conditions – such as not allowing the Greyhound to race on a professional basis – and, in many cases, it also states that if, for any reason, the Greyhound needs rehoming, he must be returned to the adoption agency.

PREPARING FOR THE NEW ARRIVAL

Before your Greyhound comes home, you must make certain preparations to ensure that you are ready for the new arrival.

Choosing Equipment

Dogs do not need a lot of equipment, but there are a number of items you will need to purchase.

Bed and Bedding

Greyhounds love their creature comforts, and it

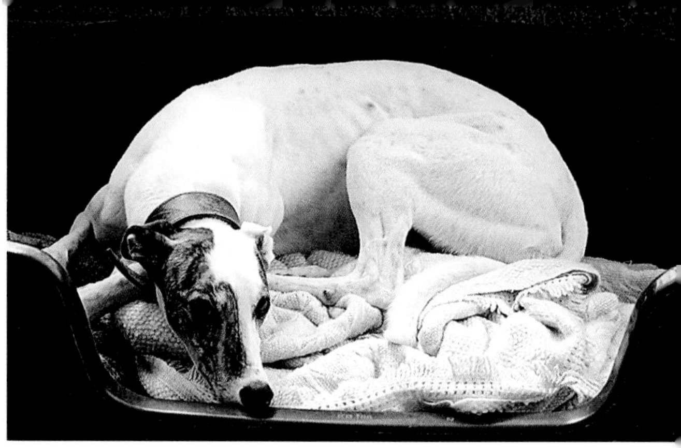

Your Greyhound will need a comfortable bed to sleep in.

is important to provide a suitable bed for your retired racer. Greyhounds have fine coats and angular bodies, and it seems that their main aim in life is to find somewhere comfortable to lie. Any self-respecting Greyhound will see the sofa as the ideal place, but you may have other ideas (see House Rules, page 57). In any case, it is a good idea to provide your Greyhound with his own bed where he can feel safe and secure.

There is a huge variety of different dog beds on the market, ranging from bean bags to wicker baskets. The most durable is undoubtedly an oval-shaped plastic bed. This is easy to clean, and can be lined with machine-washable fleece bedding.

However, it is very difficult to find a bed that is big enough for a Greyhound to stretch out. A good substitute is to provide a duvet (single bed size), with some old covers. The duvet can be moved easily, it can be machine-washed, and your Greyhound can scratch around to make his own bed, and then stretch out in luxury.

Indoor Crate

Indoor crates or kennels are now a popular option with many pet owners. A dog can be left in his crate when you go out or when you are too busy to supervise him. Ex-racers are used to being in kennels, and, in the United States, individual crates are the standard accommodation. Many dogs will have traveled to the race track in a crate, so your Greyhound will be quite happy with the concept. The other advantages are that a crate can be used when traveling in a car (see Car Travel, page 45), and, if you are going away, you can take your Greyhound's crate and provide an instant home away from home.

The one drawback is finding a crate that is big enough for an adult Greyhound to lie out in comfort. Inevitably, this size of crate represents quite a hefty investment, and, if you have limited room in the house, you may struggle to accommodate it.

Feeding Bowl

You will need two large bowls, one for food and one for water. Stainless steel bowls are virtually indestructible and are easy to keep clean. Make sure you get bowls that are big enough for a Greyhound – a size of nine inches (23 cm) in diameter is ideal.

Collar

The Greyhound has a thin neck compared with most other breeds, and so you will need a "Greyhound" collar, which is designed to fit his physique. It is wide in the middle, tapering to narrow ends at the fastening. In the United States, this is known as a martingale collar, and it is generally made of soft, nylon fabric. In the UK, most Greyhound collars are made of leather.

Lead

A strong leather lead, approximately one inch (2.5 cm) in width and 4 to 6 ft (1.22 to 1.83 cm) in length, is ideal for a Greyhound. This will give you control and allow your Greyhound to walk on a loose lead by your side.

An extending lead, which allows greater freedom, may be a useful purchase. But it is probably wise to wait until your Greyhound has settled in, as you and your dog will need some practice before trying it out in public.

Identity Disc

Your Greyhound may have his own personal ear tattoos, which were his means of identification when he was racing, but these will be of little use in his new home.

All dogs must wear some means of identification, and this is particularly important for adult dogs that are being rehomed. Inevitably, they feel unsettled to begin with, and you do not want to risk losing your dog in the early days, before he realizes where home is and who his owners are.

An engraved disc bearing contact details is a must, but you might also consider getting your dog microchipped. This is a small implant that can be scanned to reveal the dog's details. Implanting the microchip is a very simple procedure, which can be carried out by your vet.

Muzzle

Your Greyhound will be used to wearing a muzzle, and so it may be worth having one on hand to use in the early stages of training. This

A muzzle will be useful in the initial stages of training and socialization.

is particularly important if you are introducing your Greyhound to a cat, or any other small animal, when he first arrives home. (See page 51 for more information.)

Coat

Greyhounds are pretty hardy, but most will appreciate a waterproof coat in the worst of the weather. These are usually fleece-lined to provide additional warmth. Again, your Greyhound will probably be used to wearing a coat (he will certainly be used to wearing a racing jacket), so he will not put up any objections.

Grooming Equipment

The Greyhound's fine coat is easy to maintain, but it will benefit from regular brushing. A bristle brush will get rid of dried mud and loose hairs. A rubber grooming mitt or rubber curry comb can be used for a general massage.

You will also need to buy nail clippers for keeping your Greyhound's nails in trim. The guillotine type are the easiest to use (see page 68), but, if you are worried about clipping the nails, you can use a nail file or a grinder, and file the tips of the nails.

Your Greyhound's teeth will also need regular attention. A variety of canine toothpastes are available, and you can apply the paste using either a finger brush or a longer toothbrush. (See page 68.)

PREPARING YOUR HOME

Nothing is safe if a puppy is about, and new puppy owners have to go through the house making sure anything that is valuable – or hazardous – is out of reach. An adult Greyhound may not be so mischievous, but most will never have been in a home, and some may be destructive to begin with. The adoption agency will give you advice about what precautions to take when the home visit is made.

Locating the Bed

Every dog needs a place to call his own, where he can rest undisturbed. Regardless of whether you plan to use a crate, a dog bed, or a duvet, you will need to find a suitable place to locate it.

Depending on your circumstances, the kitchen or the utility room may end up being the best place, but your Greyhound will probably need closer human contact when he first arrives home.

The place where your Greyhound sleeps should be warm in winter and cool in summer, and, most important of all, it must be free from drafts.

Upstairs, Downstairs?

You may decide that it is better to restrict your Greyhound so that he does not have free access to the whole house. A stair-gate (designed for toddlers) provides an ideal barrier to stop a dog from going upstairs or for shutting off a room.

The Yard

It is vitally important that your yard is securely fenced (see The Home Visit, page 34) so that there is no chance of your dog getting out. Check also that there are no poisonous plants that your dog can nibble (your garden center will advise).

It is also a good idea to allocate an area that is to be used for toilet purposes. This helps with your Greyhound's house-training, and it is more hygienic if there is a specific area for this purpose. Of course, it is important to keep the area scrupulously clean.

Make sure the yard is fully secure, with strong, high fencing, before your Greyhound arrives home.

Car Travel

Most racing Greyhounds are used to traveling, although they may be more familiar with a van or truck than a car. They are generally accommodated in individual crates, and so, if you can fit your car with something similar, your Greyhound will adapt without any problem. If you do not wish to invest in a crate, you should fit a dog guard in the rear of the car. This keeps the Greyhound in his allocated space, and he will be able to stretch out and travel in comfort.

Finding a Veterinarian

Your Greyhound will arrive with a clean bill of health. The adoption agency will give you detailed information if there are any specific health issues relating to a racing injury, or any other condition. However, you will need to find a vet for routine care, such as booster vaccinations, worming programs, and flea treatments (see Chapter 8).

During his racing career, your Greyhound may well have been treated by a veterinarian who specializes in the care of racing dogs. This type of vet has an in-depth knowledge of Greyhound physiology and will probably have all the latest forms of equipment for treating racing injuries. This level of service is not necessary in the case of a retired Greyhound, but, ideally, the vet you select should have some experience with treating Greyhounds.

Ask the adoption agency to recommend a veterinarian, or telephone the vets in your area and find out who is likely to be the most suitable.

CHAPTER FOUR

SETTLING IN

The big day arrives when it is time to collect your Greyhound. The house is ready, the yard is secure, and you have been given a Greyhound that seems most likely to fit in with your lifestyle. What happens next?

Fortunately, most adoption agencies give an excellent support service, so you do not need to feel as though you and your Greyhound have to face a new life without any help. Most agencies will give a couple of contacts so that there is always someone you can get in touch with, and most ask if you will telephone the next day so that you can discuss any settling-in problems.

COLLECTING YOUR GREYHOUND

This part of the day's proceedings will usually go without a hitch. Racing Greyhounds are used to traveling; they often associate a journey with arriving at a track and racing, so they will be keen to get going. Ideally, you will have some type of crate or dog guard fitted in the rear of the car. Once your Greyhound knows where he is meant to go, he will hop in and settle down. Make sure he has some comfortable bedding, and you will probably hear nothing more from him until you arrive home.

If it is a hot day, make sure the car is well ventilated, and, if the journey is a long one, make plenty of water stops and allow the (adult, vaccinated) dog to stretch his legs.

If possible, arrange to collect your Greyhound in the morning, and try to keep the day free from any other arrangements. Your Greyhound will then have the whole day to get used to his home before settling for the night.

ARRIVING HOME

In the vast majority of cases, a racing Greyhound will not know of any environment except the kennels and the racing track. He will never have been inside a house and will have absolutely no knowledge of family life. Greyhounds who have spent a period of time in

Most Greyhounds will have no experience with living in a family.

a foster home will have gained some experience, but their knowledge of the world will still be very limited.

When you first arrive home, try to "think Greyhound," and see things from your dog's point of view. Do not overwhelm him by making a huge fuss and inviting all your neighbors and friends around to meet the new arrival. Your Greyhound needs a chance to take things in, to meet the family he is going to live with, and to be given reassurance as he tries to adapt to his new life.

To begin with, take your Greyhound into the yard. Give him a chance to sniff around and to relieve himself before taking him into the house. Before your Greyhound comes into the house, check that the television is not blaring, or that the washing machine is not going at full tilt. Your Greyhound will have enough to take in without added alarms.

This is the time when the individual personality of your Greyhound will be most apparent. The bolder, more outgoing type may well be bewildered when he first comes into a house, but he will be ready to explore. An excitable dog may get hyped-up by the new surroundings and will need to be calmed down and reassured. There is also the timid type who loses confidence when confronted with a new situation and will shrink away from all forms of contact.

The way you deal with your Greyhound obviously depends on the individual reaction. The best plan is to adopt a calm, confident manner. Your Greyhound is looking to you for guidance, so don't go overboard on the sympathy or your Greyhound will start to think there really is something to worry about!

It is a good idea to keep your Greyhound on the lead to start with, so that you have some control over where he goes. Remember, he will be unused to slippery surfaces, such as a kitchen floor covered in tiles or linoleum, so take things at a steady pace. Show your Greyhound his bed, give him a chance to sniff it, and encourage him to lie down. Do not make an issue of it, but, if your Greyhound lies down on his bed, stroke him and praise him. It is important that your Greyhound learns from your tone of voice when he is doing the right thing. Then go into the

Even the television can seem alarming to a dog who has never set foot inside a house.

living room and sit down quietly for a few minutes with your Greyhound at your side. Give him a chance to take things in, and then give him lots of encouragement. A Greyhound loves to be stroked, and this physical contact will also give reassurance.

Work around the house, showing your Greyhound his new home. He may not have encountered stairs before, and this can be quite a daunting prospect. Do not leave your Greyhound to try to negotiate them himself. He could easily panic and injure himself. Keep him on the lead, and walk just ahead of him. Climb a couple of steps, and then turn and face him. Encourage your Greyhound to follow, and give lots of praise when he responds. Going downstairs is potentially more hazardous, so take plenty of time, pausing every couple of steps. This is an exercise you should repeat on a daily basis. Do not allow your Greyhound free access to the stairs until he is completely confident.

To begin with, your Greyhound should be supervised at all times in his new home. In the United States, where racing dogs are used to living in crates, it is recommended that the newly adopted Greyhound starts by having a series of short periods outside his crate each day. As the Greyhound settles, he spends longer outside his crate, until he is "weaned" from it, and it is only used during the night and for times when you are away from home.

MEETING THE FAMILY

Your Greyhound may have met the members of his new family when you were visiting the rehoming kennels. But it is a good idea to start from scratch once your Greyhound arrives home, so that you can supervise introductions.

Keep your Greyhound on the lead, and allow each member of the family to come up and meet him. Let the Greyhound sniff each person so that he learns their scent. He also needs to hear everyone's voice in turn, so that he starts to recognize his family.

In most cases, adoption agencies are reluctant to rehome Greyhounds with small children (see page 28). There should be no problem with older children who can be instructed to be calm and sensible. Let everyone stroke the new arrival, but guard against overwhelming him with too much manhandling and too much attention. Your Greyhound is bound to feel very tense, and too much fuss may do more harm than good.

When your Greyhound has had a chance to meet everyone and explore his new home, bring his bed into the room where you plan him to be. Show him his bed, and give him a chance to

After your Greyhound has explored his new environment, he will settle down.

settle. Continue reading the newspaper or peeling the potatoes, quietly ignoring him. Hopefully, this will give your Greyhound a chance to relax for a little while, but he will still have the comfort of your presence.

THE RESIDENT DOG

Your Greyhound will have been tested with other dogs before being placed in a home that has a dog, but it is important to handle the first meeting between the resident dog and the newcomer with tact. The resident dog is likely to feel threatened, and this could easily lead to an aggressive response.

The best plan is to introduce the two dogs on neutral territory. You will need an adult member of the family or a friend to help you do this. It may be safer to muzzle both the dogs to begin with. Keep both dogs on the lead, and give them a chance to sniff each other. They need to communicate with each other in canine language, so do not interfere unless one of the dogs shows aggression. If this happens, give a sharp tug on the lead and reprimand the dog so it is clear that this type of behavior is unacceptable.

Go out for a walk so that the dogs have a chance to get to know each other, walking together calmly. When you return home, make sure that both dogs are closely supervised for the first couple of days. If you are using a crate, it will be a useful way of giving the dogs some quality time apart. If you are going out, you should separate the dogs until you are sure you can trust them both.

If you supervise initial introductions, your Greyhound will soon accept the resident dog.

Test your Greyhound every few days to make sure he is 100 percent cat-safe.

Watch your own reactions closely. If you become tense, it may well have an adverse effect on the dogs' behavior. Treat each animal without fear or favor, and you will soon establish canine harmony.

MEETING THE CAT

Again, your Greyhound will have been cat-tested before being placed in a home with a cat. But you must take the greatest care with initial introductions. Even if your Greyhound has been labeled as "zero" prey-drive, he should still be treated cautiously when interacting with other pets. Occasionally, a dog that exhibited no interest at all in a cat during the test, may, when he begins to feel comfortable and more sure of himself, start to show some chasing behavior. It is best to introduce a Greyhound to a household as though he is high prey-drive and to continue to monitor the dog's behavior, using a muzzle and leash and positive reinforcement (praising and giving treats for good behavior) as long as necessary to ensure that the dog and cat can live together safely.

Never introduce a Greyhound to a cat outside the house. This would be asking for trouble as the cat has the opportunity to run, and, almost inevitably, the Greyhound will chase. Start off in the house with your Greyhound on the lead and muzzled. It is important to make sure on this, and all future, occasions that the cat has an escape route. For example, doors should be left open and stair-gates can be used to prevent the dog from going upstairs.

Ask an adult member of the family or a friend to gently hold the cat on the floor. Do not attempt to make the introduction when the cat is being held in someone's lap. Allow the Greyhound to sniff the cat, making sure that the cat's claws are kept well out of reach. Walk the dog away, and see if he is willing to move on to other things, or whether he is intent on getting back to the cat.

Some Greyhounds will try to bite the cat through the muzzle, some will try to pound the cat with their paws, and there are those that will practically pull your arm out of its socket in an attempt to get at the cat. If the Greyhound appears to be obsessed with the cat and will not be distracted, this is a sure sign that he is not cat-safe. Unfortunately, very few of these dogs can be trained out of this behavior.

If the Greyhound sniffs at the cat and wags his tail, he is generally just showing interest. To begin with, this should be kept in check. Give a gentle, corrective tug on the collar, say "No," and walk the dog away. Hopefully, he will go with you rather than pulling to get back at the cat. It may take a few tries before you achieve the desired result.

Some Greyhounds are actually afraid when they meet the cat. The dog may whine or back away. Usually this type of dog remains wary of the cat, but sometimes, when the dog is more relaxed in his new home, he may become more assertive. To be safe, retest every few days for the first week or so until you are positive that the dog is cat-safe. Greyhounds can be very fast at "dispatching" their prey. A quick snap of the jaws, or coming down hard on a cat's spine, could be fatal. So take no chances.

No prizes for guessing who is going to win this race! Some Greyhounds are surprisingly tolerant of small animals, but never take unnecessary risks.

ENCOUNTERS WITH SMALL ANIMALS

A Greyhound has to be fairly exceptional to live alongside small animals such as rabbits and guinea pigs. But there are those that have done it. To begin with, muzzle your Greyhound and keep him on the lead. Allow him to go up to the hutch or cage and sniff. If he shows any interest, correct him, and then walk away. If the dog shows any excitement, you are probably on a loser. It is highly dangerous to test the situation any further. If you have a very placid Greyhound and your small animals are kept in secure accommodation, well out of reach, your Greyhound may learn that these particular members of the family are out of bounds.

For the first few weeks, you will need to re-test your Greyhound several times a day. You must also ensure that your Greyhound does not have free rein in the house when you are out. If you have small animals of any kind, it is far safer to keep your Greyhound in a crate when you are not there to supervise him.

HOME SWEET HOME

Denise Dubarbier and her husband Michel, who live in Streatham, a suburb of London, had always owned Cocker Spaniels. But when the oldest of her three dogs died, her children, Claire, Eve, and Michael, who were then in their early teens, persuaded her to adopt a Greyhound. This was the start of a whole new career for Denise, starting as a home-checker and fund-raiser for retired Greyhounds, and now working in rehoming kennels. Her two Greyhounds, Jake and Lulu, are registered therapy dogs.

"I had seen Greyhounds walking in the park, but I didn't know anything about them," said Denise. "I had this image of a racing dog in a muzzle, and I was concerned that this sort of dog would turn on the spaniels – let alone the guinea pig...

"Fortunately, the home-checker spent a lot of time with me and was able to reassure me. He brought his two Greyhounds with him, so I was able to get an idea of the size of them in the house, as well as seeing that they were fine with my dogs.

"There were a couple of dogs in the rehoming kennels that he thought would be suitable, so we went along with the spaniels. We looked at one Greyhound who seemed quite sweet, and then Jake came out, and wagged his tail at the children. He was so handsome and so pleased to see us.

"We took him for a walk with the spaniels and he was amazing. He completely ignored them, and then when we let the spaniels off the lead in the paddock, he was absolutely fine with them.

"We took Jake home, and he was so good from day one, I thought: 'This can't last,' but it did. He was so laid-back, he took everything in his stride. He was no trouble with the spaniels, but I was worried about what he was going to make of the guinea pig.

"At that time the guinea pig was in a run in the garden. I had Jake on the lead, and I also had him muzzled. He went up to sniff at the run, and then he saw the guinea pig move. He pulled towards it, and I was very firm with him, telling him 'No,' and checking him.

"I spent the afternoon sitting by the run with Jake on the lead. Every time he tried to get at the guinea pig, I told him off.

"Greyhounds are very sensitive and hate being disapproved of, so soon Jake got fed up with

Jake performing his party trick of hide-and-seek.

HOME SWEET HOME ▶

HOME SWEET HOME

It took Lulu no time to settle in her new home.

being told off. He learned he was not allowed to go near the guinea pig, and we never had any trouble with him from then onwards."

Within a year of getting Jake, Denise had started working as a home-checker for retired Greyhounds. Four days before Christmas, she was asked to go and collect a Greyhound whose home placement was not working out.

"We were told that the Greyhound kept stealing the children's toys and thieving from the kitchen bin. She was also unreliable with her house-training.

"I couldn't bear to put her in kennels over Christmas so I said I would foster her for a few days and try to find out what the problem was."

Lulu, a white and black Greyhound, fell on her feet. As soon as she proved that she could get on with the spaniels, Denise could not bear to give her up.

"She was clearly stressed to begin with, and I thought we were going to have a difficult couple of days," she said. "But the first night, I put her to settle on a blanket, and she was still there when I came down the next morning.

"She hadn't made a sound, and she was perfectly clean. I think she was just the type of Greyhound who needed other dogs around. Now she's a real diamond."

HOUSE-TRAINING

Many new owners fear that house-training is going to be a major problem for a dog that has spent all his life in kennels. In fact, all the hard work has already been done – you just need to do the fine-tuning.

Any animal hates to soil his own bed, so a Greyhound that is kept in a kennel will try very hard to keep his sleeping quarters clean. In racing kennels, the Greyhounds are let out at regular intervals in their runs, as well as having free exercise in the paddocks, so they have plenty of opportunity to relieve themselves.

When Greyhounds are put up for rehoming, an extra effort is made to let the dogs out on a routine basis – such as every two hours – to encourage them to be clean. However, when your Greyhound arrives in his new home, do

Stick to a routine of trips out to the yard, and your Greyhound will soon get the idea.

not expect him to behave like the average house-trained dog, attracting your attention when he wants to go out, or scratching at the door. To begin with, you will have to do the thinking for your Greyhound.

Keep a check on the time, and make sure that you let your dog out at regular intervals. Go to the area in your yard you have allocated for toilet-training, and stay with your Greyhound until he has performed. It is useful to use a command such as "Be clean," so that your dog will learn to associate the command with the action. Praise your dog lavishly, and then go back into the house.

The bonus of taking on an adult dog is that he will be quite capable of going through the night without needing to be let out. Physically, a puppy cannot be expected to do this, and so "accidents" at night are an inevitable part of house-training until the puppy becomes a little older. If your Greyhound has the opportunity to go out last thing at night – and is not fed too late in the evening – there should be no problem.

If you work hard at house-training when your Greyhound first arrives home, you will be amazed at how quickly he gets the idea. Do not become complacent too soon; keep letting your Greyhound out every two hours during the day, and then he will not be forced to make a mistake in the house.

If you are using a crate, you will find that this helps the house-training process. The Greyhound will naturally be clean in his crate, and, with regular trips out into the yard, he will soon get the idea.

For advice on inappropriate toileting, see page 88.

THE FIRST MEAL

Your Greyhound will probably have had his breakfast before leaving the kennel, so you will need to feed his main meal. It is a good idea to give your Greyhound the diet he has been used to in the kennel and to try to stick to the same timetable – at least to begin with. Changes should be kept to a minimum until your Greyhound has had a chance to settle.

Do not be surprised if your Greyhound refuses his first meal, or just picks at it. A Greyhound has to feel relaxed in his surroundings in order to eat – and this may take a day or two. If your Greyhound leaves his meal, pick it up, and discard it. You can try offering him a fresh meal a little later in the day. Make sure there is fresh drinking water readily

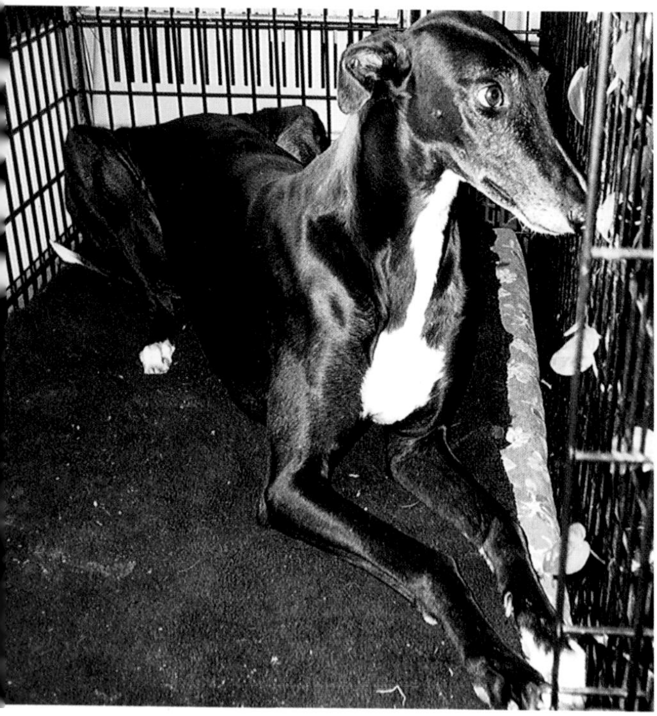

In the United States, Greyhounds are used to crates, and this helps the settling-in process.

available, and do not worry unduly. Your dog will not suffer if he goes on a self-imposed diet for the first day or two. If the problem persists, seek expert advice from the adoption agency, or consult your vet.

THE FIRST NIGHT

Most people would expect a puppy to cry the first night he is in his new home. He will miss the warmth and comfort of sleeping with his littermates, and he will be upset because his human family appears to have deserted him.

It is much the same for a Greyhound spending his first night in a new home. Obviously, in kennels, the dogs are used to being left, but they are in a familiar environment and surrounded by other dogs. In the UK, where a pair of Greyhounds are usually housed in the same kennel, the dogs have constant canine companionship.

For the newly adopted Greyhound, the first couple of nights can be traumatic. Suddenly, the lights go out, the people vanish, and the Greyhound is left in an environment where he feels strange and insecure. It is hardly surprising that he becomes anxious and starts to bark or whine.

There are two schools of thought when it comes to dealing with this. There are those who feel the dog has got to learn to be alone, and the sooner he does so, the better. And there are those who take a more flexible approach, and try to ease the Greyhound into his new situation. The problem with trying to be strict with your Greyhound is that it can be entirely nonproductive. The Greyhound becomes more and more stressed, and has no idea of what is expected of him. The new owners suffer sleepless nights, become increasingly irate, and soon they are at the end of their patience. All too often, adoption agencies get cries for help from owners who say that their Greyhound simply will not settle. Yet all this heartache could easily be avoided.

Some owners are quite happy to allow their Greyhound to sleep in the bedroom – some even allow the dog on the bed! Obviously, these dogs will have no problem settling. But, if this does not fit in with your arrangements, there is a halfway house. Instead of shutting your Greyhound in the kitchen or utility room, move

Establish house rules at an early stage so that your Greyhound knows what is permitted.

his crate or his bed outside the bedroom door. The Greyhound will not feel abandoned, and he will start to understand and accept the family's nighttime routine.

Allow your Greyhound to learn a step at a time. If you are anxious to move him into the kitchen/utility room, do not let him sleep outside your bedroom one night and then shut him up on his own the following night. Move the bed or crate a little further away every couple of nights. Perhaps, during the daytime, you can leave your Greyhound shut in his sleeping quarters for a short period before releasing him. In this way, he will learn to trust you, and he will learn to relax in his surroundings.

Within a couple of weeks, most Greyhounds will be perfectly happy to be left alone.

HOUSE RULES

Although you do not want to nag your Greyhound from the moment he arrives home, it is sensible to work out some house rules so that he can learn what is, or is not, acceptable behavior. Again, you must bear in mind that your Greyhound has absolutely no idea of what is right or wrong, so there is no point in getting angry or shouting at your dog. He will just be completely confused and may well lose his confidence as he fails to understand what is required.

First of all, make up your own mind about appropriate behavior. You may be quite happy for your Greyhound to lie on the sofa – and it will certainly be his preferred option – but, if you would rather this did not happen, you must be 100 percent firm and consistent. Do not ignore him one moment, and then come down on him like a ton of bricks the next. If you want to stop your Greyhound lying on the sofa, tell him "No" in a firm voice, and take him to his own bed. Encourage him to lie down, and then give lots of praise. If this is repeated, in the same firm but fair manner, your Greyhound will soon understand that the sofa is a no-go area.

The kitchen is a wonderfully exciting place for a kennel dog who has never previously been in the presence of so many enticing smells. There is the smell of cooking, the scent of food left out on kitchen surfaces, and the fascinating smells coming from the wastebasket. It is little wonder that a Greyhound can get carried away and may try jumping up to get at the food, or have a go at scavenging in the trash. Your Greyhound has no moral sense that he is stealing. As far as he is concerned, he is merely taking what is on offer.

To re-educate your Greyhound, you will need to catch him red-handed. Tell him off: say "No," sounding gruff and disapproving, and then command him to "Leave" so that you can take away his stolen goods. In time, your Greyhound will learn that your gruff tone of voice means that his behavior is unacceptable. He must do the right thing, responding to "Leave," to win your approval again.

This being said, the best course of action is to be vigilant so that your Greyhound is not left unsupervised in the kitchen, and also to work at clearing food away so that it is not left out as a temptation. Your Greyhound will learn to respect your wishes when you are in attendance, but he may never be entirely trustworthy. Most owners of Greyhounds have a tale to tell about disappearing food – and, with an uncanny sense of timing, it usually happens just before you call a party of guests in for dinner!

In the first few weeks after your Greyhound arrives home, it may seem that you are saying "No" all the time – your dog could be forgiven for thinking that "No" is his new name. However, it is important to define the boundaries of good behavior so that your Greyhound understands what is expected. The golden rule is to be firm, fair, and consistent.

Start by taking your Greyhound out in a quiet area so that he can get used to the outside world.

THE OUTSIDE WORLD

Socialization is regarded as the key element when you are rearing a puppy. This is a process of educating a youngster so that he becomes entirely familiar with the world he is living in. Ideally, socialization starts from a very young age, often when the puppy is still with his mother and his littermates. The breeder will handle the puppies, and, as the pups get a little older, they will be allowed to explore their environment.

When the puppy goes to his new home, he will absorb all the sights and sounds of an ordinary household; he will get used to the washing machine, the vacuum cleaner, the radio, and the television. When the pup has received full protection through his inoculations, he will be taken into the outside world. Gradually, he will become accustomed to the hurly-burly of crowds and traffic, and he may be taken on a train or a bus. He will get used to loud noises, such as roadwork, and then go to the park where he will meet other dogs and see children playing. A young puppy soaks up new experiences like a sponge, and by the time he reaches adulthood, he should be a well-balanced individual who is able to cope with any situation he encounters.

Compare this with the life of a racing Greyhound. During the highly significant learning period, a Greyhound has scarcely any contact with the outside world. This is the time when he is being given the freedom to run and gallop, so that he can develop into a finely tuned racing machine. In adulthood, the racing Greyhound knows of no other life beyond the track and the kennels. He will probably be well socialized with people, but, in every other way, the newly adopted Greyhound is like an alien arriving on a new planet.

If your Greyhound has spent some time in a foster home, he may have started going out and about, but there will still be many situations that he has never encountered. Do not tax your Greyhound too much to begin with in an effort to make up for lost time. Start off gradually, perhaps going for a short walk on a fairly quiet street. Your Greyhound should be wearing his martingale collar (see page 43), and you must check that it is securely fastened. It must also be correctly fitted – allowing two fingers inside the collar when it is fastened. A collar that is too tight will be uncomfortable; a collar that is too loose could easily be slipped if your Greyhound gets into a panic.

Racing Greyhounds are used to walking on the lead so, with a little verbal encouragement, you should be able to step out without any problem. If your Greyhound appears to hesitate, stop, and give him a chance to have a second look at whatever is worrying him. In most cases, Greyhounds simply need a little time to adjust. The next time you go out, try a short trip in the car followed by a walk in the park. This will teach your Greyhound that walks are fun, and he will also have the opportunity to see other dogs. If there is a play area, you can allow your Greyhound to watch children playing and he will be able to get used to the sound of their voices.

In no circumstances should you be tempted to let your Greyhound off the lead. Your dog scarcely knows you, he has had no formal training to come when he is called, and, as a former racing dog, he is more than likely to chase after the first moving object he catches sight of.

There are lots of ways to exercise your Greyhound safely (see page 70), but, in the first few weeks, keep him on the lead at all times. This does not mean that he has to spend every outing walking to heel on a short lead. It is important that your Greyhound has a chance to sniff and to take in his surroundings.

Growing Confidence

As your Greyhound grows in confidence, you can take him to increasingly busy environments. As before, give him a chance to stop and look at anything he is suspicious of, and give lots of praise and encouragement when he walks on again. Sometimes your Greyhound may find something really alarming – the noise of air-brakes is a classic. Respond calmly, showing your Greyhound there is nothing to worry about and encouraging him to go forward. Never try to force your Greyhound to go past something he is frightened of. This will have an entirely negative effect, and the dog may lose his trust in you. This would be highly detrimental at the beginning of a relationship when the Greyhound is learning to look to you for guidance. It is important that your Greyhound sees you as his leader and knows that you are there to look after him.

If your Greyhound is frightened of something, do not go out of your way to avoid it on all future occasions, just because your dog showed initial fear. Go back again and again so that he learns there is nothing to fear. However, you should only do this in short spurts, and never more than once a day.

Give your Greyhound a chance to take in his surroundings.

LEAVING YOUR GREYHOUND

It is strongly recommended that you keep your commitments as light as possible when your Greyhound first arrives home. Your dog needs a chance to get used to you and to start feeling secure and unthreatened in his new environment. However, it is also important for your Greyhound to learn that he can be left without feeling that he has been totally abandoned. It is natural for him to feel nervous to begin with, because being left is a completely new experience for him. But do not assume that your Greyhound has separation anxiety. With time, and with plenty of encouragement from you, your Greyhound will learn to overcome his initial fear.

This lesson starts when you leave your dog for the night (see page 56), but your Greyhound also needs to understand that there is no cause for alarm if he is home alone. This is particularly important if you go out to work, and your Greyhound is going to be left for a reasonable period each day.

The best plan is to ease your Greyhound into what is going to be your workday routine. Leave your Greyhound for a short length of time, and then build on this gradually. Start by leaving your dog for ten minutes, then, after a few hours at home, go out for about fifteen minutes. Over the next week, go out for longer periods.

When you are back at work, never leave your Greyhound for longer than four hours. If you work longer hours, it is essential that you return home for at least an hour to see your dog and to exercise him. If this is not possible, you will need to use the services of a dog-sitter.

For advice on separation anxiety, see page 87.

ESTABLISHING A ROUTINE

A Greyhound is far more likely to adapt to his new home if he understands the routine and knows what to expect. Obviously, you cannot become a slave to routine. It is not always possible to feed your dog at exactly the same times each day, and there will be days when you have to change your schedule for walks.

However, dogs, and particularly Greyhounds, are creatures of habit. They will soon learn to get excited when a walk is due or to settle down when you have to go out. So it is in your interests, particularly to begin with, to find a routine that suits you and to try, within reason, to stick to it.

Dogs have a very efficient internal body-clock, and your Greyhound will soon be nudging you with his nose, politely informing you that it is time for his dinner.

THE SETTLED GREYHOUND

The length of time it takes for a Greyhound to settle into his new home depends very much on the personality of the dog.

The timid type will need sensitive handling, and it may take some time before the dog starts to relax and show his character (see page 92). The bolder Greyhound will superficially adapt more quickly, but it is important to remember that all Greyhounds, regardless of individual behavior patterns, have a huge amount to learn.

In the majority of cases, adopters find that the most significant settling-in period is within the first two weeks. During this time, the Greyhound's horizons are broadened. He learns to trust his new owners, he realizes that, if he is left for a period of time, he is not being abandoned – and he discovers that there is a lot to be said for living in the real world as a companion dog!

ALL'S WELL THAT ENDS WELL

Rosemary and Steve Turner wanted a dog, but as they have two children – Kerry-Ann, aged nine, and Ann-Marie, aged seven – they were anxious that it should be 100 percent sound in temperament. They started looking in local dogs' homes, but they found nothing suitable. Then, on a trip to Cambridge, they visited an animal shelter and saw a Greyhound – they were instantly smitten.

"The dog was standing on his own, looking so lonesome. I immediately thought: 'I want one of them'," said Rosemary.

In fact, that particular Greyhound was not available for rehoming. The Turners live in Plymouth in the southwest of England, which is some distance from any big Greyhound tracks.

"We decided to use the Internet," said Rosemary. "We logged on, and found a rehoming agency."

Rosemary and Steve made the long trip to visit the kennels, and looked at the dogs awaiting adoption. They took an immediate liking to Al, a white and fawn dog, aged two years.

"He was very quiet, with beautiful, sad eyes," said Rosemary. "We took him out for a walk and he was nice and calm. He also seemed quiet with the other dogs."

Although most Greyhounds are used to traveling, Al was car-sick on the journey to his new home, and he arrived in a sorry state.

"We were up all night with him," said

Al: The ideal family companion.

Rosemary. "He kept being sick, so we just gave him a little water to drink. The next day, I didn't feed him and his stomach settled down."

FAMILY WELCOME

Al was introduced to the members of his new family on the lead, and he appeared friendly and confident.

"My sister has rehomed two dogs, so my children were used to being sensible with dogs," said Rosemary. "They just came up and stroked Al, and then left him in peace."

The first meeting with the family parrot was a little more eventful. Al went up to the cage and was bitten sharply on the nose.

"He has never been near the cage since," said Rosemary. "He completely ignores the parrot, in spite of all the noise he makes."

Al found the house a very bewildering place to begin with.

"We have parquet floors in the hall and in the kitchen, and Al doesn't like them at all," said Rosemary. "He finds them very slippery, so he tries to avoid walking there. He is a very quiet dog; the only time we have ever heard him bark was when he caught sight of his own reflection in the television screen."

House-training caused few problems. Al had a couple of accidents to begin with, but when he was changed to a complete diet that had a lower moisture content, he was completely clean.

SEEING THE WORLD

Al gets most of his exercise from accompanying the two children to school in the morning and collecting them in the afternoon.

"He was worried by the traffic to begin with," said Rosemary. "I noticed that he was especially concerned when the traffic was coming towards us, so for the first few days I crossed the street so we walked with the flow of the traffic. He was okay with that, so then I tried him again with the cars coming towards us. He was a little bit hesitant, but then he decided it was all right and he has been fine ever since."

Al has met other dogs at the school and in the park, but he has been kept on a lead and muzzled, to be on the safe side.

"He seems a bit frightened of the bigger dogs, and he has taken rather an interest in a little West Highland White Terrier – but he tends to whine at them rather than pull to get at them," said Rosemary.

Al had been in his new home four weeks, and he is settling in well to his new lifestyle.

"He is absolutely brilliant with the children," said Rosemary. "They come and sit with him, and he just puts his head in one of their laps and lies there to be stroked. The only time he gets excited is when the children come home. He likes to be in the same room as me, but he is quite happy to lie sleeping. He doesn't even bother to get up when someone comes to the door."

So what is the verdict on adopting a Greyhound?

"We all love him – he's the ideal dog for us," said Rosemary. "In fact, Steve is so keen, he's already making plans to adopt another Greyhound...."

CHAPTER FIVE

CARING FOR YOUR GREYHOUND

There is a common misconception that Greyhounds are difficult to care for. People think a former racing dog will need a special diet and a complicated exercise regime, and they fear that old injuries may flare up.

In fact, the Greyhound is a straightforward, low-maintenance breed that should live to a ripe old age with few serious problems. However, it is important to understand the specific needs of a Greyhound so that you can give the care and attention that is required.

FEEDING

During their racing career, Greyhounds are fed a top-quality, high-protein diet. This often consists of meat and vegetables soaked in a gravy, with brown bread or biscuit. Some kennels now feed complete diets, but the traditional method of feeding is still favored by many.

In a home environment, it is not always convenient to be boiling great pans of meat and vegetables, and it can also prove to be an expensive diet to feed. More importantly, the retired Greyhound is living a completely different life; his body no longer has to contend with the demands of racing. It is therefore sensible to change the diet to one that is better suited to a companion dog.

There is a wide variety of dog foods available, and Greyhounds will adapt to most types. So it is a matter of finding the diet that suits your Greyhound, your lifestyle, and your pocket. Some canned foods can be too rich for a Greyhound's digestion and may lead to stomach upsets. If you opt for a complete diet, make sure that you do not choose one that is high in protein. A retired Greyhound is not using up the energy that this type of diet requires, and the dog may become hyped-up in his behavior. Some Greyhounds have even become destructive when fed an incorrect diet. Pet food labels give an analysis of the nutrients that are contained, so check this out, and, if necessary, seek advice

To begin with, try to feed the diet your Greyhound is accustomed to.

from your vet as to what food is likely to be most suitable for your Greyhound.

For the first few days, feed your Greyhound whatever he has been used to. If you introduce a new diet, do so gradually, adding the new food a little at a time. Make sure that you do not increase the overall ration, but, over a period of a few days, you can substitute the diet. Keep a close check on how your Greyhound responds to the food. Evidence of diarrhea or flatulence is a sign that the diet is not suitable. If this happens, do not immediately swap to a new diet, or you may make the situation worse. Consult your veterinarian, and ask him to recommend a new feeding program.

The manufacturers of dog foods give guidance on the amount to feed, and this is calcuated in terms of a dog's weight. In the case of a retired Greyhound, it is helpful if you know your dog's racing weight. As a rule of thumb, the retired Greyhound should be 4.4 lb (2 kg) heavier than his racing weight.

If you do not have this information, it is a matter of assessing your Greyhound's condition to see if he is being fed the right amount. Although the Greyhound has a slim build, he should not be skinny. You should not be able to see the pin bones on his back, but you should be able to discern the three lower ribs. Conversely, obesity should also be avoided at all costs as it seriously endangers a dog's health.

Greyhounds should be fed twice a day – some seem to do better if their ration is divided into three small meals. Cool, fresh water should be available at all times, particularly during hot weather. (See Chapter 8.)

GROOMING

The Greyhound's fine, sleek coat is easy to care for, but this does not mean that you should forget about grooming! Perhaps the most important aspect of grooming is that it gives you the opportunity to give your dog a thorough check-over.

If there is a problem, which could be anything from a small bald patch to a lump or a swelling, you will detect it in the very early stages. This makes treatment easier, and the outcome is far more likely to be successful.

A bristle brush will loosen the dead hair.

A racing Greyhound is used to a routine of daily grooming and massage so you will find that your adopted Greyhound is easy to handle. Most dogs enjoy the attention, and your relationship with your dog will improve with this kind of daily interaction.

Coat Care

Most Greyhounds will stand to be groomed, and their height means that the task is not too back-breaking. Many trainers stand astride the dog when they are grooming and massaging, and this method certainly helps you to reach all parts of the body with ease.

Start by using a bristle brush. This will get rid of dried mud and will help to loosen dead hair. Work from the front of the body, brushing the chest and neck, and then proceed down through the body to the hindquarters. Then use a hound glove or rubber currycomb, and start the process all over again, this time using a massaging action. This has the dual benefit of taking out loose hairs and massaging the muscles. To finish with, use a dry towel or a piece of velvet to rub the coat. This is not essential but it brings out the sheen in the coat so that your Greyhound looks in top condition.

When you are grooming your dog, keep a close check for any evidence of external parasites, such as fleas or ticks. (See Chapter 8.)

A rubber currycomb can be used for massage as well as for grooming.

Ears should be checked to make sure they are clean and smell fresh.

If nails grow too long, they will need to be clipped.

Ears

Check the ears as part of your daily routine. They should be clean, with no discernible odor. Do not attempt to probe into the ear canal with cotton swabs; you will almost certainly do more harm than good. If there is dirt on the inside of the ear, this should be cleaned using a little olive oil on a wad of cotton-wool (cotton). If the ear seems very mucky and foul-smelling, your Greyhound may have ear mites, or he could be suffering from an ear infection. In both cases, consult your veterinarian who will prescribe the appropriate treatment. (See Chapter 8, page 120.)

Feet and Nails

Examine your dog's feet to make sure that the pads are not cracked or sore, and that the nails are not growing too long. It is a relatively simple matter to trim the nails, but, to begin with, it is advisable to enlist the help of an experienced Greyhound owner or to ask your veterinarian to do the job.

The nails can be clipped with guillotine nail clippers. It is important to trim the tip of the nail only. If you clip back too far, you will cut the quick (the nerves and blood supply of the nail), which will bleed. The quick can be seen in white nails, but not in black nails, so it is better to err on the side of caution and trim just the tip of the nail. Some people prefer to use a nail file. The job takes longer, but there is no danger of cutting back too far.

Teeth

Teeth should be checked every couple of days, and, if there is any evidence of tartar accumulating, they will need to be cleaned. You

Teeth can be cleaned with a finger brush.

can use an angled toothbrush or a finger brush to work in the canine toothpaste. It is very important to do this regularly as neglected teeth can quickly lead to decay and gum infections.

If possible, allow your Greyhound to gnaw on a marrowbone. This is the best way of keeping teeth clean, and the dog derives a great deal of pleasure from it. A marrowbone is the only safe bone to provide, and the dog must always be supervised. (See Chapter 8.)

Bathing

Fortunately, the Greyhound's short coat does not attract a lot of mud or dirt, and, as a breed, they do not seem to have a very doggy smell. Bathing can therefore be limited to an annual or twice-annual event – unless your Greyhound decides to roll in anything unspeakable!

It is probably easiest to bath your dog in a shower stall. If this is not possible, the good-natured Greyhound will submit to being lifted into the bath without a great fuss. Make sure that you place a nonslip mat in the bath or shower so that your Greyhound can get a firm footing.

The secret of bathing a dog is to have everything ready in advance – otherwise chaos reigns... You will need shampoo (one that is made for dogs), conditioner (this is optional), a plastic jug, and a pile of dry towels. Before bathing, you can plug your dog's ears with cotton-wool, so that no water can get in.

- Soak the coat thoroughly with tepid water.
- Apply the shampoo and massage into a rich lather. Make sure that you do not get shampoo into the eyes or ears.
- Take great care when rinsing out the coat to ensure that there is no trace of shampoo remaining.
- If you are using a canine conditioner, dilute it in a jug, and then pour it over the coat.
- Again, rinse the coat thoroughly.
- Before you allow your Greyhound to get out of the bath or shower, take a towel and absorb as much of the excess moisture from the coat as possible.
- Fasten a lead, and then take your Greyhound outside for a good shake.
- The coat should then be towel-dried before grooming.

TEMPERATURE CONTROL

Greyhounds have thin skins and fine coats,

A pale Greyhound may be prone to sunburn.

which are both great assets to an animal running at speed, but they can be a drawback for the companion dog. If the weather is very cold or very wet, your Greyhound will appreciate wearing a coat. There is a huge variety of coats, specially designed for Greyhounds, so you can choose whatever is the most suitable. Greyhounds are used to wearing coats, so you will have no problem persuading your dog to wear one.

At the opposite extreme, Greyhounds feel the heat, so it is important to make sure that your dog does not become overheated. Never leave your Greyhound in a stationary car; even on an overcast day, the temperature quickly builds up. A dog can die from heatstroke in a remarkably short space of time, so take no risks.

If you have a white or pale fawn Greyhound, he may be prone to sunburn along the top of the nose and at the ear tips in hot weather. You can use a sunblock cream on these sensitive areas, or else restrict the amount of time your Greyhound spends outside in these conditions.

EXERCISING YOUR GREYHOUND

Greyhounds do not need a lot of strenuous exercise, but, ideally, three walks a day should be part of their regular routine. The walks do not have to be very extensive, but a short outing in the morning, in the middle of the day, and in the evening will keep your dog fit and will provide interest and variety in his life.

Adoption agencies advise that retired Greyhounds be kept on the lead in public places. However, if you keep up a reasonably brisk pace, you and your Greyhound will both benefit. Try to vary your outings, sometimes walking on roads, and sometimes in the park. This will help with your Greyhound's socialization, and he will not become bored with the same surroundings. Road-walking also helps to keep the nails in trim and the feet in good condition.

It is a good idea to train your Greyhound so that he is used to walking on an extending lead. Practice in the yard, so that you know how to operate it, and your dog gets used to walking at some distance from your side. Do not use an extending lead in the street, as an accident could easily happen if the lead is accidentally released to its full extent.

The bonus of using an extending lead in the park is that it gives your dog a controlled amount of freedom. Every dog needs the

EXERCISING YOUR GREYHOUND

Greyhounds will enjoy exercise on the lead, but if you have the opportunity to allow your dog to run free in a safe place, you will be rewarded with a magnificent display of canine athleticism.

opportunity to sniff and to "just be a dog" without being corrected or restrained on a short lead. However, you must remain vigilant when your Greyhound is on the extending lead, particularly when he first arrives home. A Greyhound has extremely good sight, and he can pick up a moving object that is a considerable distance away. The lead could be pulled out of your hand, and so it is a good idea to use a wrist strap as an added precaution.

Stepping Up the Pace

A Greyhound who walks well on the lead can easily step up a pace and get greater benefit from his outings while still remaining on the lead. If you are fit, why not try taking your Greyhound with you when you go out jogging? With a little verbal encouragement, your Greyhound will run alongside you, but will not attempt to pull ahead.

Free-Running

If your Greyhound is getting two to three regular walks a day, he will not suffer if he does not have the opportunity to run free off the lead. Although it is wonderful to see a Greyhound galloping at full stretch, the opportunities to provide this type of exercise safely are very limited. However, Greyhound owners are an inventive breed, and there are ways of getting around this problem.

Many parks now have specially designed dog walks, and these are perfect for the retired Greyhound. They are always enclosed, and provide a short running stretch or circuit that will be free from children, joggers, and any other potential hazards. If you use a dog walk on a regular basis, you will find out the quiet times when there are the fewest number of dog walkers.

If you have a Greyhound who is not reliable with other dogs, you can arrange to wait your turn and to make sure that your Greyhound has a free run when no other dogs are present.

Some Greyhound owners have fenced yards or have access to fenced facilities. It is also worth finding out if there is a fenced athletic ground in your area, which may allow the exercising of dogs at certain times.

In the United States, groups of Greyhound owners get together for supervised dog play periods. The Greyhounds are always muzzled, as a number of dogs of any breed running together could cause problems, but both dogs and owners get a lot from these outings. If you live near a Greyhound rehoming kennel, you can probably make arrangements to exercise your dog in the paddocks.

Clean Up!

As a responsible dog owner, you must always pick up after your dog in public places. In many cases, hefty fines are imposed if you fail to do this, but, at all events, it is the only civilized behavior that is acceptable in the community today. Before you go out, make sure that you have a plastic bag or a "pooper scooper" with you. In most parks, disposal bins are provided.

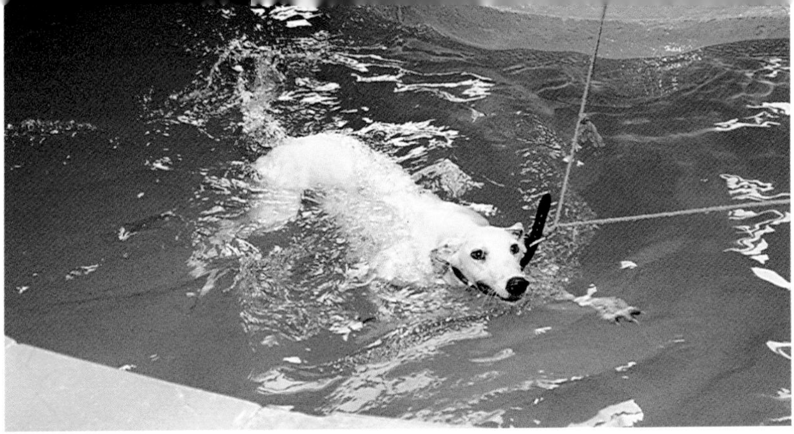

Swimming is of particular benefit to Greyhounds with muscle injuries.

Swimming

Swimming is a very natural form of exercise, and it has proved to be of great benefit in improving muscle strength in injured Greyhounds.

Some Greyhounds will have exercised in swimming pools during their racing days, and, given the opportunity, they are happy to re-use their aquatic skills. Some Greyhounds need more encouragement, and others have absolutely no intention of getting their feet wet!

If your Greyhound shows a liking for swimming, check that conditions are safe before allowing your dog to take the plunge. Strong currents are a danger, and you must also make sure that there is an easily accessible place for your dog to get out. Make sure that you know what's beneath the surface of the water before allowing your dog to dive in (many rivers are littered with rusting shopping carts, broken glass, etc.).

When you go on a swimming expedition, make sure that you take a towel with you so that you can dry your dog thoroughly. If swimming in the sea, make sure that your Greyhound is rinsed thoroughly (especially his pads which can become sore and cracked if the sand and salt are not removed).

There is an increasing number of special dog swimming pools, which allow you to exercise your dog safely.

A Mad Five Minutes

Everyone who has ever owned a Greyhound will tell you of the times when their dog has suddenly taken it into his head to have a mad five minutes. All at once your gentle, sedate Greyhound transforms into a top racer, speeding around the house or yard as if it were an oval-shaped track. Showing his skills of old, the Greyhound bends and twists around any obstacles that get in his way, acting as though he were a puppy on his first schooling run. Then, just as suddenly, the Greyhound returns to couch potato mode – and his mad five minutes is nothing but a breathless memory.

THE AGING GREYHOUND

There is no set time when a Greyhound starts to show his age. As they are not the most energetic of breeds, taking things a little more slowly can be almost indiscernible. However, between 10 and 12 years of age, you may find that your Greyhound is slightly stiff when getting up; his hearing may not be so acute and perhaps his eyesight is a little dimmed.

These are perfectly normal signs of old age, and your Greyhound will continue to enjoy his life as much as ever. Keep a check on exercise, particularly if you are lead-walking, and make sure that you do not go further than your Greyhound is happy with. If the weather is cold or wet, be extra-considerate. Your Greyhound will appreciate wearing a coat, and, if he does get wet, make sure that you dry him when you return home.

Dietary needs may well change as the metabolism slows down. There are now many excellent complete diets specially formulated for the veteran dog, and you may find that this suits your Greyhound.

Older dogs tend to sleep more, so allow your Greyhound to rest undisturbed, particularly if you have small children in the house. But do not be so concerned as to exclude your dog from family activities. A dog is a pretty good judge of his own capabilities – so, if your Greyhound wants to have an energetic spell, let him go ahead.

Do not look on the last few years of your Greyhound's life as something to dread. It is a precious time when you can really enjoy the company of an old friend.

LETTING GO

Sadly, the time will come when your Greyhound has reached the end of his life. Sometimes a dog will die in his sleep, but more often a health problem is diagnosed, and, eventually, the moment comes to put a stop to the dog's suffering.

This is the hardest decision a dog owner ever has to make, and it is one about which you have to be completely unselfish. We would all like to keep our dogs alive as long as possible. But if your beloved Greyhound is in pain and is getting no enjoyment from life, you must face the inevitable.

It will take time to get over the loss of your dog, but try to take comfort from the memories of the happy times you have spent together. You can never replace a dog, but the greatest tribute to your Greyhound will be to take on another former racer who is desperately in need of a loving home.

This 12-year-old Greyhound is still fit and active.

THE GIFT OF LIFE

Newman's story is unique. He was retired from racing, but just a couple of months after being adopted he became seriously ill. He had acute kidney failure, and, if he didn't get treatment, he would die within weeks.

Nicole Timbrook who lives in New Jersey, already had two adopted Greyhounds at home, and she volunteered as a foster parent for a Greyhound adoption group. Perhaps, most importantly, Nicole was a veterinary surgical technician and anesthetist, and so she had specialized knowledge in caring for sick animals. She took over Newman's case, and, thanks to her tireless efforts, she gave him the gift of life.

"His name was Newman. I never did find out what his racing name was, and it didn't seem to matter," said Nicole. "He was a big, muscular white dog with brindle patches, and big doe eyes that made me melt when I looked into them. On the car ride to the hospital where I worked, I tried tempting him to eat. I tried some french fries, a bit of hamburger, but he refused everything. It broke my heart – when a dog stops eating, it is usually a bad sign.

"When we got to the hospital, there was a battery of diagnostics that had to be done: an abdominal ultrasound to look at his kidneys, an echocardiogram to see if he had any heart disease, and renal blood panels to determine how damaged his kidneys were. Newman's kidneys were failing rapidly, and we were going to have to be aggressive in his treatment if he was going to live. Fortunately for Newman, our practice was new, and he was one of our first 'in-hospital' patients. We were able to give him a lot of attention over the next few weeks.

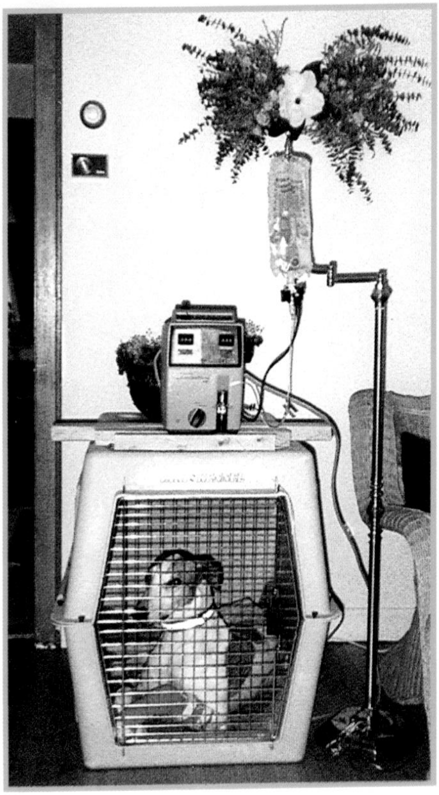

Newman in his makeshift hospital in Nicole's home.

"At that stage, we did not have overnight staff, and Newman needed treatments and fluids throughout the night. I packed up all his medications and took him home for the night. I made a makeshift hospital in my living room, fixing the fluid pump on top of his crate, and using a lamp stand as a fluid hook. I set my alarm clock to go off every two hours throughout the night so that I could take him outside, collect and measure his urine output, and adjust his fluid rate accordingly.

"This routine went on all through the week and over the weekend. If I needed to go somewhere, Newman, his fluid pump and medications would come with me. I would hang the fluids from a hook in the car, and he would lie quietly on the seat. Every time I needed to give him medication or check his urine output, we would pull over and take care of it. We must have been quite a sight. But Newman never once gave me an ounce of trouble. He was the perfect patient.

"Newman's kidney values started to improve slowly day by day. The first time he ate an entire meal and kept it down, I was jumping for joy. But the turning point was when I took him out of his

THE GIFT OF LIFE ▶

run to walk him, and I had a toy in my hand. Newman literally jumped 2 ft in the air to grab the toy! That was when I knew he was a fighter, and I couldn't let anything happen to him.

"By this time, the results of the blood tests had come through. It was determined that the cause of Newman's renal failure was a disease known as Leptospirosis. It will never be known how he contracted this disease, but at least we knew what we were up against. After six weeks, the fluid therapy was finally discontinued."

A SETTLED HOME

"Newman's renal values were better – not perfect – but he had a chance of living a reasonably normal life for a little while. I knew that the damage done to his kidneys would one day get the better of him, so I thought it was unfair to ask anyone to adopt him. I therefore asked if I could adopt him.

"Newman came to live with me permanently and joined my other two Greyhounds to become a pack of three. Over the next two years there would be flare-ups of his kidney disease, which would require administering fluids under the skin, but what I got in return was the most playful and loving dog that I have ever known. Newman seemed to relish life. He would run around the yard playing tag with the other dogs, jumping up for his toys and throwing them in the air. He loved to go to the river and run into water up to his chest. When it was a quiet night at home, he would lay on the couch with his head in my lap, or just lean up against me when I was making dinner as if to say 'I'm still here.' But most of all, he would smile. I had heard that a lot of Greyhounds smile, but I had never seen it before. He would close his eyes halfway, peel back his lips so you could see his teeth and move his head from side to side. You couldn't help but be in love with him when you saw that!"

A CRISIS LOOMS

"It was almost two years to the day when Newman's condition started to decline. I didn't want to lose him so I again became aggressive with his treatment. He went back on to intravenous fluids, and we also had to treat him

Enjoying life to the full with Nicole's two other Greyhounds.

for anemia. I was so attached to Newman that I couldn't bear to leave him in the hospital overnight, so, again, I would pack up all his things and take him home for treatment. I felt fortunate that, because of my medical training, and the wonderful people I work for, I was able to spend as much time with Newman as possible.

"As the end neared, Newman started refusing food. I began cooking all sorts of tempting treats for him, and some days he was better than others. If he ate a meal I was elated, other days I had to keep from sobbing when he wouldn't touch the roast beef that I offered him."

LOSING THE BATTLE

"As the weeks wore on, I knew he was losing the battle. I was preparing myself for the inevitable, but yet I just couldn't seem to let go. I had worked so hard to give him as close to a normal life as possible, and there had been so little time since he retired from racing. I just wanted him to feel love for a little while longer.

"Everyone at work was very supportive. They knew that I would make the final decision, on my own, when I felt it was right.

"The day came when Newman was so weak that I had to help him to go outside. He had refused to eat for the last 36 hours, and I couldn't let him starve to death. I knew that the time had come.

"I let him get comfortable on his big sofa bed, and pulled a blanket over his thin body. He looked so peaceful – I knew he wanted to rest. I sent the other dogs out to play, and turned on some soothing music. Because he already had an intravenous catheter in for his fluids, it was very easy to inject the euthanasia fluid as I talked softly to him and said goodbye.

"It was a very quiet and peaceful end. I lay down next to him for a little while, and then let the other dogs in so that they would understand that Newman had passed away. They seemed to understand what had happened, and curled up on the couch with me as if to try to console me.

"Once I got myself together, I called a veterinary practice that had its own crematorium. I brought his body to them. When I left him there I felt such an ache in my heart that I knew I had to do something to remember him by.

"I had seen a plaque at a local store, and for some reason, I knew the inscription would remind me of Newman's courageous spirit. I went out and bought the plaque and placed it above my front door. Every time I walk through that door, I look at it and smile, just like Newman would do every time you came home from a long day at work."

UNCONDITIONAL LOVE

"I was fortunate because I was able to take care of Newman's illness myself, with the help of the specialists I work with. The average person has to depend on their veterinarian to help them get through this difficult time.

"I think that grieving for a pet is natural and healthy. They give us such unconditional love, how can we not give our all to them?

"The people who can help most are those who have been through the same sort of experience. They need to be animal-people; non-animal-people don't seem to comprehend the emotions involved in caring for such wonderful creatures.

"It also helps if you have other dogs at home. They redirect your attention and keep you looking forward to coming home at the end of the day. You know they will be there, ready to show you their love, and waiting to receive love in return."

CHAPTER SIX

TRAINING TARGETS

You may not be planning to train an Obedience Champion – but everyone wants a well-behaved dog that they can be proud to own. Those who adopt a former racing Greyhound are not starting out the easy way. If the puppy is equated to a blank piece of paper ready to be filled with positive experiences, the retired Greyhound corresponds to a hefty book, with most of the pages torn out. We are in no doubt that an ex-racer has a history, but we know little about it. His behavior will have been shaped and influenced by what has happened during his lifetime, but we can only deal with the dog as he presents himself.

Before you even attempt to train your retired Greyhound, be realistic.

- You are dealing with a sighthound whose chief motivation is to hunt and chase.
- Your Greyhound will have received little or no training in canine good behavior.
- Your Greyhound will have had a very incomplete education in terms of socialization, and so he may have irrational fears and suspicions.

This all sounds very negative, but identifying the problem is the key to tackling it. On the plus side, you will have a dog that is sound in temperament and docile by nature. A Greyhound will never be desperate to please, like some Border Collies for example, but most will be eager to win your approval.

STARTING RIGHT

All dogs must be motivated to obey – and this means that there must be something in it for them. Reward-based training is now generally accepted as the most effective method for teaching dogs – a far cry from the days when harsh treatment and punishment were seen as the way forward.

With a Greyhound, you need to find out what constitutes a reward. The majority of dogs will do anything for a food treat, although some breeds respond more positively to a training toy. Experiment with your Greyhound and see what

interests him most. Make sure that the food treat is something special – a piece of cheese or cooked liver are perennial favorites. It has to be perceived as a real treat that is worth working for.

A training toy can be anything that your Greyhound enjoys having a game with. This can be a ball on a rope, a tug toy, or a soft toy. Some trainers use the dog's lead and let the dog have a game with it after each exercise is finished. Whatever you choose, make sure that you put it to one side and only use it when you are training. This means that the toy has special value, and the game is viewed as a top reward.

CLICKER TRAINING

This method of training, which is based on sound association, is becoming an increasingly popular way of working with animals. The clicker is a small plastic box, which, when pressed with the thumb, makes a "click." This signals a correct response and tells the dog that a treat is coming. Eventually, the sound of the clicker becomes a reward in itself.

The advantage of the clicker is that you can reward your Greyhound the instant he responds correctly. It is a "yes" marker, telling the dog he is performing well.

Lines of Communication

Your voice and your body are two great aids for training – and the big advantage is, you always have them with you!

Use your voice to issue commands. These should be short, clear, and consistent. If you want your Greyhound to go into the Down position, the command is "Down" – not "Lie down" or "Go and lie down." Your Greyhound is reacting to the sound of the word, not the meaning, so if you keep changing the command, you will end up with a very confused Greyhound.

Your voice is also used as a means of reward, to praise your dog when he has responded correctly. Be lavish with your praise, making your voice sound warm and encouraging. A Greyhound is not used to this form of communication, and so you must make it crystal clear when you are pleased with him, so that he learns to listen for verbal praise.

It is also helpful if you have a release command, such as "Okay," that you give when an exercise is finished. This means that your Greyhound is allowed to break position, and he has earned his treat or his toy as a reward.

Dogs rely a lot on body language as a means of communication. If you observe two dogs meeting each other, you will see clear signals that are given out by their body posture. A dog standing tall, with his ears pricked and his tail held high, is taking on a dominant, assertive role. The dog with his ears back, body held low to the ground and tail between his legs, is showing that he is inferior and submissive.

When you are training, your dog will observe your body language in order to pick up clues as to what he is meant to do. Be positive in your actions. For example, if you command "Wait," hold your palm facing your dog like a barrier. If you command "Come," open your arms to welcome your dog.

Do not forget the physical praise – stroking him and cuddling is a reward for good behavior.

Training Environment

When you start training your Greyhound, choose an environment that is as free from distractions as possible. The aim is for your dog to focus his attention on you, so it is important to ensure that there is nothing more interesting to attract his attention. The yard is a good place for training, as long as you have it to yourself and there are no outside disturbances. If you have enough room, you can also work in a room or in a corridor in your house.

Distractions (such as someone walking past) should be added later in the dog's training, once he has a full grasp of the commands. This will prepare him for life in the outside world, and ensure that he will reliably obey you, wherever he is.

TRAINING EXERCISES

Sit

The Sit exercise is not a great favorite with Greyhounds. Their conformation does not allow them to sit comfortably – you very rarely see a

"Sit" is never a favorite with Greyhounds, but most will respond if a reward is offered immediately.

Greyhound sitting by choice. However, it is a relatively easy lesson to teach, as long as you do not expect your dog to stay in position for too long. In the early stages, you may find it easier to work with your Greyhound on the lead so that you have greater control.

1. Select a tasty food treat or training toy and show it to your Greyhound. Hold the treat/toy just above your dog's nose, so that he looks up at it.

2. In order to balance himself as he looks up, your Greyhound will start to lower his hindquarters and, with luck, he will go into the Sit position. If you are using a clicker, click the instant your dog goes into the Sit. You can introduce the verbal command "Sit" when your dog is confidently going into the correct position.

3. If there is some hesitation, apply gentle pressure on your dog's hindquarters to encourage him to sit.

4. When he responds correctly, click, give him the treat, and praise him quietly in that position. Then give the release command, and, if you are using a training toy, reward him with a game.

You can also teach this exercise at mealtimes, holding the food bowl just above your Greyhound's head. This usually works wonders, as your dog has a really big motivation for doing as you ask.

The Down is one of the most useful exercises to teach.

Down

The Down exercise is an extension of the Sit, and it comes much more naturally to Greyhounds.

1. Use a treat/toy, and lower it to the ground. Close your hand so that your dog knows the treat is there, but cannot get it.

2. To begin with, your dog will lower the front half of his body to try to get at the treat. When he finds this is to no avail, the back half will come down so that he is balanced and can concentrate on getting at the treat.

3. As your dog goes into the correct position, click and reward. When he is regularly going into the position you want, introduce the verbal command "Down."

4. Stroke him gently so he stays in place until you give the release command, followed by his treat.

Wait/Stay

The Wait/Stay is the most important lesson you can teach your Greyhound – it could even be a lifesaver in an emergency.

1. Start with your Greyhound on lead. He can be in the Sit, the Stand, or the Down – whichever position he is most likely to stay in.

2. Hold your palm flat, facing your dog, and step away two paces. Click if the dog stays in position.

3. Pause for about 15 seconds, and then return to your dog's side. Praise him quietly before giving the release command, and a treat.

4. Gradually increase the distance you leave your Greyhound, and build up the amount of time you ask your Greyhound to wait. You can use a training line – a cord approximately 9 ft. (2.75 m) in length – so that you can leave your Greyhound at a greater distance.

5. When you are confident that your Greyhound fully understands the exercise, work on it off-lead.

6. Finally, practice the exercise from a variety of different positions. If your Greyhound has been practicing the Wait from a Down position, teach him the command from a Sit and a Stand, etc.

In an emergency situation, many owners rely on an instant response to the "Down" command, as a means of stopping the dog in his tracks. However, with Greyhounds, it seems that "Wait" elicits a more immediate response. It is certainly a lesson that is well worth teaching.

Come

To begin with, the Come exercise should be practiced in the yard, with as few distractions as possible. It is helpful if you can recruit a member of the family or a friend to help.

1. Start off with your Greyhound off the lead, and your assistant holding on to the dog's collar. Show your Greyhound that you have a treat or a toy, and then walk some distance from him.

Build up the Wait or Stay command in easy stages.

2. Turn and face your dog, and then call him enthusiastically: "Blaze, come." As you give the command, open out your arms to encourage him to come to you.

3. When your Greyhound responds, click, give lots of praise, and reward him with a treat or with a game.

When you are first teaching this exercise, do not worry about leaving your Greyhound in the Sit, or getting him to Sit when he comes to you. You are looking for a swift response to the verbal command.

The secret of a good recall is that the dog wants to come to you. He must understand that responding to "Come" always means a treat and lots of praise.

If you are able to allow your Greyhound off-lead, be prepared to work even harder at getting a good response when you are competing with outside distractions. If your dog is a bit slow coming back, try running off in the opposite direction – that usually motivates the dog to follow you.

Never scold your Greyhound when he comes back to you – no matter how long he takes. Dogs live in the present. Your Greyhound will not understand that you are scolding him for a slow response; he will think you are cross because he has come to you.

Retrieve

Greyhounds are not natural retrievers, and, if your dog is not interested in playing with toys, you will struggle to teach the exercise. This is of no importance, as retrieve is far from being an essential exercise; it is just a way of interacting with your dog and enhancing your relationship.

1. Start by playing with the training toy and get your Greyhound really focused on it.

2. As your Greyhound takes the toy in his mouth, click and reward.

3. Let him hold the toy and then take it back.

4. Introduce a command for taking the toy ("Hold") and a command for giving it up ("Give"), so that your Greyhound learns that he is allowed the toy but must give it up when you ask for it.

5. The next step is to throw the toy so that your Greyhound has to run out to retrieve it. As you throw the toy, give the command "Hold" or "Fetch," and encourage your Greyhound to go and get it. To begin with, you may need to run with him and kick the toy around, so that he is interested in it. Click as soon as your Greyhound is holding the toy.

6. You can then introduce the recall: "Blaze, come." Do not snatch at the toy as he comes to you, or your Greyhound will think that you are spoiling the game. Let him hold it for a moment, and then command "Give." When your Greyhound responds, click, and reward with lots of praise.

THE RETRIEVE

The Greyhound is not known as a retrieving breed – but some dogs show a natural aptitude.

If your Greyhound is determined to run off with his toy, attach it to a length of rope. Keeping the end of the rope in your hand, throw the toy and command your Greyhound to "Hold." When he picks up the toy, command "Come," and give a gentle tug on the rope. Your Greyhound will quickly realize that you have control of the toy, and you can encourage him to bring it to you by winding in the rope.

It will take some time to get your Greyhound retrieving on command, but your patience will pay off. Remember, retrieve is a fun exercise that both you and your Greyhound should enjoy.

TRAINING CLASSES

As your Greyhound becomes more settled, you may consider attending training classes at a local club. This will help with your dog's socialization as well as his training.

Do not rush off to the nearest club without checking it out first. Attend a couple of club meetings, without your Greyhound, and watch a training session in progress. You are looking for instructors who use positive forms of training, based on reward. It is also important that the instructor understands Greyhounds, and will treat them sympathetically, with reasonable expectations of what they are likely to achieve.

SOLVING PROBLEMS

In most cases, a retired Greyhound will adapt to his new life within a matter of weeks. Of course, he will still go on learning as he encounters new experiences, but you will have established a relationship of trust, and your Greyhound will have learned to respond to you.

Unfortunately, some dogs find the adjustment from kennel life harder to make, and their sense of insecurity may be expressed in a number of different behavior patterns, ranging from excessive barking to being destructive in the home. It is important to remember that these dogs are not being deliberately bad. They are simply reacting to the panic, confusion, or bewilderment they are feeling.

With time and understanding, most Greyhounds who suffer from this type of anxiety can be re-educated to stop their deviant behavior and learn to come to terms with their new situation.

THE DESTRUCTIVE GREYHOUND

There is nothing worse than returning home to find your dog has been busily occupied with wrecking the place. An adult dog can do a lot of damage, and you are left feeling angry and frustrated, not knowing how to stop the cycle of inappropriate behavior.

What Can You Do?

The first step is to find out if there is a physical cause for your Greyhound's behavior. If a dog is fed a diet that is too high in protein, he may become overactive, and this could lead to destructive behavior.

Seek advice from your veterinarian or from the adoption agency. It could be that your

Some Greyhounds become destructive because they are worried about being left on their own.

Greyhound is not getting enough exercise, or perhaps you are leaving him on his own for too long.

If a physical cause is ruled out, you will have to attempt to re-educate your Greyhound. There are two ways of dealing with destructiveness, and they should be attempted simultaneously. First, you must prevent your Greyhound from being destructive. Second, you must try to find the cause of your dog's anxiety which is leading to his deviant behavior.

Prevention

Invest in a crate (see page 42). This may be expensive, but if you have a destructive dog on your hands, you will find that it is well worth the investment. If your Greyhound is confined, there is nothing for him to wreck.

When you leave your dog unsupervised, make sure that he is wearing a muzzle. This is no hardship to a former racing dog, and it obviously limits his opportunities to misbehave and may prevent injury to the dog.

A crate is not a cure for destructive behavior. It is simply a way of preventing it, in the short term, during those brief times when you cannot supervise your dog. In the meantime, the source of the problem behavior should be investigated.

Finding a Cure

It could be that your Greyhound is panicking when he is left on his own, and he is giving vent to his feelings by being destructive. The use of the crate means that your Greyhound cannot be destructive. If he is not accustomed to using a crate, you need to train him to accept being left for short periods. If necessary, a Greyhound can be muzzled to stop him from gnawing the bars of the crate.

- Most Greyhounds are happy to go in a crate. If your dog shows any reluctance, feed him in the crate, leaving the door open, so that he will learn to associate his crate with a pleasurable experience.

- Line the crate with comfortable bedding, and, to begin with, try leaving your Greyhound for short periods of around 30 minutes while you are still in the house.
- If your Greyhound shows signs of anxiety, ease him into times of separation even more gradually. Start off sitting in the same room with him and then going next door.
- When you need to go out, try leaving your Greyhound in his crate with some appropriate things to chew on. Try filling a hollow, sterilized marrowbone with some peanut butter or some cheese; your Greyhound will have hours of fun trying to extract it. You can also buy boredom-busting toys. These are specially designed blocks or cubes in which you can secrete food treats.
- Gradually build up the amount of time you leave your Greyhound in his crate. Try leaving a radio with the volume switched on low. Your Greyhound may feel more settled if he is not left in silence.
- Get another canine companion, one who is calm and confident. Good behavior is often contagious, and some dogs become nervous without the company of another dog.
- If the problem behavior persists, seek the immediate advice of a pet behavior counsellor.

Summary

The key to your Greyhound's anxiety is that he feels abandoned when he is left. In time, he will learn to trust you, knowing that you will return. The crate not only stops the dog from being destructive, but it also provides a safe haven where he can feel secure until you return.

INAPPROPRIATE TOILETING

House-training rarely causes a problem (see page 54) if you supervise your Greyhound carefully when he first arrives home. However, some Greyhounds continue to make "mistakes" in the house, long after the initial settling-in period.

What Can You Do?

The first task is to find out if there is a physical cause for your Greyhound's lack of cleanliness. If, for example, your dog has a urinary infection, incontinence may well result. Ask your veterinarian to give your Greyhound a thorough check-over.

If your Greyhound has a clean bill of health, you will need to look at other possible causes. It could be something very simple, such as not allowing your Greyhound sufficient opportunity to go out in the yard before leaving him. Your Greyhound may feel threatened by his new environment (see page 92), or, in the case of a dominant animal (male or female), it may be a way of marking new territory.

Trial and Error

Be extra-vigilant with your Greyhound, letting him out at least every 90 minutes. Go out with him in the yard and stay with him until he

A crate will help the Greyhound to settle when he is left on his own.

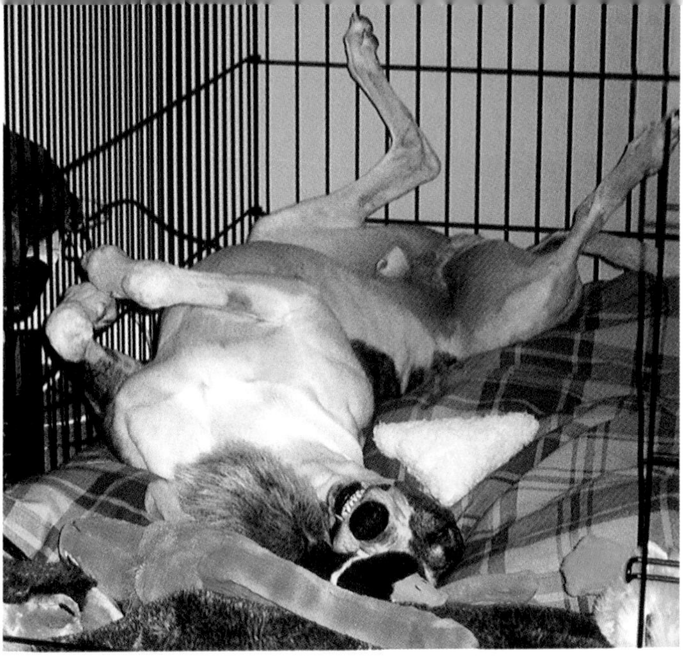

has performed. Give him lots of praise so that he knows he has behaved correctly.

- Observe your dog's behavior to see if there is any reluctance about using his toilet area. You may have allocated a grass toilet area, and your dog has been used to going on concrete – or vice versa. This may seem unimportant, but it could be enough to upset a dog and make his house-training unreliable. Retrain the dog (page 54) on a variety of surfaces (grass, gravel, sand, etc.) so that he becomes more versatile.
- A crate will also help your Greyhound to be clean. Dogs hate to foul their own sleeping quarters, so, if your Greyhound is confined (when he is unsupervised at night, for example), he will think twice before making a mess.

The Stress Factor

- Do your Greyhound's mistakes coincide with when you leave him alone? It could be that he becomes stressed and resorts to an immature form of behavior.
- Using a crate will help your Greyhound to settle when he is left alone, particularly if the length of the period for which he is left is built up gradually.
- Never punish your dog for making a mistake; you will only make matters worse.

THE MACHO GREYHOUND

If you have a male Greyhound, he may think that he needs to mark out his new territory. If you already have a resident dog, the newcomer may be struggling to prove his status, trying to show that he is top dog.

- Buy a spray, available from your vet, which can be used on the staging posts where your Greyhound lifts his leg. This will eliminate the odor, and, hopefully, help to break the habit.
- Consider having your Greyhound neutered. This will put a stop to most macho behavior. Remember, the dog's hormonal pattern will not settle down for some eight weeks after surgery – so do not expect instant results.

Summary

Finding out the cause of your Greyhound's inappropriate toileting is essential if progress is to be made. In some cases, it may be necessary to go back to basics and to start house-training all over again so that your dog fully understands what is required. In other instances, it may be that, once your Greyhound has got used to being left alone, he becomes settled and does not need to resort to antisocial behavior.

THE AGGRESSIVE GREYHOUND

Greyhounds are not aggressive by nature, and it is rare for this form of behavior to cause a problem. However, if a dog of any breed shows signs of aggression, it is essential to act immediately as a potentially dangerous situation could arise.

If a Greyhound has a tendency to be aggressive, the adoption agency will not put the dog forward for adoption. There are a few isolated cases where Greyhounds have been considered unhomeable for this reason, and they are kept on as permanent residents of the rehoming kennels. This may not seem like a marvelous option, but it is far better for the dog – and the community – that no one is put at risk.

What Can You Do?

If your Greyhound shows any hint of aggression, you must seek expert help. Ask your vet to give the dog a thorough examination to ensure that there is no physical cause. If an animal is in pain, its behavior may well become unpredictable. If there is no underlying reason, contact the adoption agency for advice, or consult a professional dog trainer or behaviorist.

It is so rare for a Greyhound to be aggressive that you must seek specialist help.

Aggression Toward Other Animals

The adoption agency will already have tested your Greyhound with other animals (see pages 37–38), so it is unlikely that your dog will suddenly show animosity toward the household pets. However, there have been cases where a Greyhound has shown no animosity toward a cat or a dog when tested, but, on arriving in his new home, he has taken an instant dislike to the resident pet.

There is no accounting for this – it could just be a clash of personalities. This situation could lead to disaster, and so it is advisable to return the dog to the rehoming agency and to try again with a more placid individual.

Summary

It is very unusual to encounter aggression in a Greyhound, but, if you see any signs of trouble, do not delay in seeking professional advice.

THE DOMINANT GREYHOUND

If a Greyhound has a dominant nature, he may try to test relationships with his new owners. He may become possessive over his bed, his food, or a toy, or he may start disobeying the house rules. This behavior should be viewed as your Greyhound pushing his luck to see how far he can go.

What Can You Do?

In order for a dog to live in harmony with his human family, he must learn to accept his inferior status. This does not mean that the dog has no rights and is pushed around by all members of the family. Your Greyhound should be respected and treated with kindness and firmness at all times. But it is essential that the dog accepts his low-ranking status and does not question your leadership.

Dominance Reduction

There are a number of ways to teach your Greyhound to respect his human family, using pack rules to communicate the dog's position in the family hierarchy.

- Always feed your Greyhound after the family has eaten.
- Command your Greyhound to "Wait" every time you go through a door, or go up or down stairs. Your dog will learn that you always go first, he always follows.

The assertive Greyhound must accept his place in the family pack. Always feed the family first, before feeding your dog.

- If you are having a game with your Greyhound, make sure that you are the one to end it, rather than allowing your dog to run off with the toy.
- Work at the training exercises outlined in Chapter 6, so your Greyhound understands he has to obey you.
- Make sure that your Greyhound only sleeps in his own bed, rather than taking over your armchair.

You can also work at the situations where your Greyhound is attempting to challenge you.

- When your Greyhound is feeding, drop a treat into his bowl, so that he learns to welcome the intrusion.
- Halfway through a meal, take the food bowl away for a moment and then replace it. Your Greyhound needs to learn that you are in charge of the food.
- When your Greyhound is in his bed, crouch down and give him a treat, then stroke him and praise him. This breaks down the barrier he is attempting to put up concerning his personal space.

Summary

There are some breeds, like Rottweilers or Bullmastiffs, that have a natural tendency to guard and to be dominant, and this has to be counteracted with positive training while they are still young. The Greyhound is not a dominant breed, but there is always an individual who may try to push his luck. If you are experiencing problems and your dog is not responding to the training program outlined previously, seek advice from the adoption agency or from a dog behaviorist.

THE TIMID GREYHOUND

All newly adopted Greyhounds will undergo a period of stress when they are settling into their new homes. For the more sensitive dog, this can be a very troubled time, which will need careful handling. The timid Greyhound is reluctant to confront new situations and new people. Anxiety is expressed by shaking and shivering, and becoming increasingly withdrawn. In extreme cases, a Greyhound may urinate out of fear.

What Can You Do?

You need to build up your Greyhound's confidence so that he is ready to face the challenges of his new environment.

- Spend as much time as you can with your Greyhound. To start with, stay at home so that your Greyhound learns to relate to you in a nonstressful environment.
- If your Greyhound is worried about being in the same room when all the family are present, do not make a big issue of it, trying to coax your dog to join you. Leave the door open, and carry on with whatever you are doing. Nine times out of ten, you will find that your Greyhound starts to inch closer. Again, just ignore your dog and allow him time to make his own decisions. Gradually you will find that your Greyhound gains in confidence and is ready to be part of the family circle.

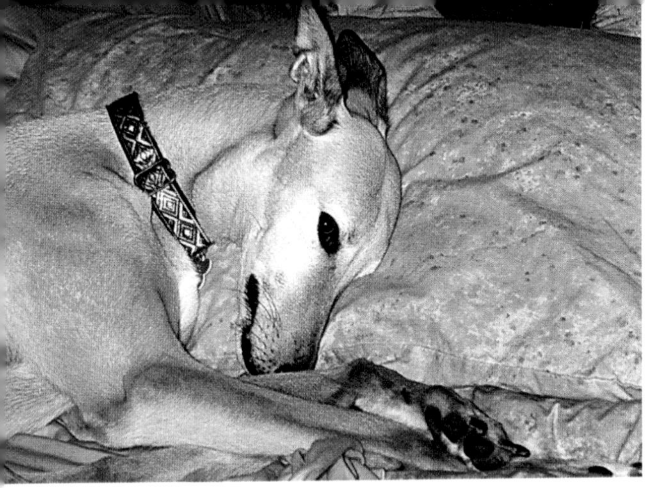

The timid Greyhound needs lots of reassurance.

- Try a few simple training exercises. Concentrate on things that you know your Greyhound can do, so that you can boost his confidence.
- As your Greyhound settles at home, allow an occasional visitor to call. Let the visitor give a food treat to your Greyhound, but make sure that the dog is not overwhelmed with attention.
- If you have a dog-friendly delivery man, ask him to give your Greyhound a treat before he comes into the house.
- On walks, adopt a calm but positive approach. Allow your Greyhound to stop and look at anything that is worrying him and then move forward briskly, perhaps using the incentive of a food treat.

Summary

Time will solve the problems of most timid Greyhounds. Make sure that you are loving and supportive, but do not fall into the trap of being too sympathetic or your Greyhound will think his neurotic behavior is justified. It is important that the Greyhound also learns to accept periods of separation, or he may become anxious when he is left alone. To begin with, leave your Greyhound in his crate for short periods. You can also use a stair-gate so that your Greyhound is on his own, but he can still see you in the adjoining room.

There are some cases when a Greyhound fails to respond to the measures outlined here, and it appears that he has a real personality disorder. If you are concerned about your Greyhound, seek the advice of a vet (preferably one who specializes in animal behavior) who may be able to prescribe some form of medication to help with the problem. This type of treatment should only be used short-term and should always be combined with the behavior modification techniques that are described here.

SEEKING HELP

The vast majority of problems that are encountered with retired Greyhounds can be attributed to the trauma of adjusting to a new life in adulthood. Within a couple of weeks, most dogs have found their feet and never look back.

Some Greyhounds need special care and understanding, and their owners will need the patience to work through the behavior patterns that may result from anxiety and insecurity. If, at any time, you feel your Greyhound is not responding to your training program, the best route is to seek help from the adoption agency or to ask your vet to recommend the services of a professional dog trainer or behaviorist.

BLOSSOMING CONFIDENCE

Paula and Robert Boswell were occasional visitors to Wimbledon Greyhound Stadium in south London. They saw a poster asking for volunteers to walk retired Greyhounds, and they started going to the kennels on weekends. They both worked full-time, and so they could not take on the commitment of owning a Greyhound, but they agreed to provide a short-stay foster home when it was needed. They were asked to take Harry home for a few days – and it changed their lives.

"When we first brought Harry home, he was a nervous wreck," said Paula. "We got as far as the hall, and he refused to move. We stood for 20 minutes, and Harry just stood there trembling. In the end, he gave in and followed us into the living room but it was three days before he would sit in the same room."

Harry had been racing at Wimbledon, but his problems started at some point previously. When he arrived at the racing kennels, he was a very nervous dog, and he was particularly frightened of men. If he saw a man wearing a cloth cap, he would back away and show real fear. At the track he was treated with kindness, but, although he was very fast, he did not have the confidence to run out on his own and win races. When he was retired, nobody wanted him because he was so nervous. He was five years old, and his future looked very bleak.

"Harry was not our first choice to foster, but the kennel talked us into taking him for a few days as they thought he would benefit so much," said Paula. "But we knew by the end of the first day we would have to keep him. We could not bear to return him to kennel life. We were very lucky as we were able to make arrangements with a friend who could take him out in the middle of the day when we were at work, and walk him with her other dogs.

The world was full of terrors for Harry when he first arrived in his new home.

"To begin with, Harry was frightened of everything. He found a corner in a back room, and he would not come out. We let him take things at his own pace, and, slowly, his curiosity got the better of him, and he would come and find us. We always had a treat to give him, and he began to accept us.

"At the time, my two sons were living at

The laid-back Harry, on vacation with the Boswells.

home as well as Robert, and Harry had to learn to overcome his fear of men. To start with, he was terrified of loud, deep voices, and he would go scurrying back to his corner. But eventually he understood that no one was going to harm him. He is fine with everyone in the family, but he is still frightened of other men."

Harry gained confidence in the house, although he has never ventured upstairs and he has never tried to get on the furniture. He also had to come to terms with living with a cat.

"To be honest, Harry was more frightened of the cat than the other way round," said Paula. "He has never tried to chase the cat, and he is always very respectful. He allows the cat to come into his bed and just makes room for him."

The outside world was full of terrors for Harry. He was worried by loud noises and was particularly alarmed if someone walked close behind him.

"Robert would take him out and he was just very patient with Harry. He didn't force him, but he encouraged him to keep going. We never felt we were alone dealing with Harry's problems; we knew we could always get help and advice from the rehoming staff."

Paula estimated that it took over a year before Harry really began to settle and his personality began to show. Now he goes on vacations with the Boswells and stays in hotels – he is every bit the family dog.

"He is the most gentle, loveable dog," said Paula. "He is still nervous, and I think he always will be. But he is happy with his family, and he loves my granddaughter – mostly because he sees her as a good source of food!

"I can honestly say that having Harry has enriched our lives. Our circle of friends has certainly widened, as we are now in touch with a lot of other Greyhound owners. We have had to be patient with Harry, but he has repaid us many times over."

CHAPTER SEVEN

HAVING FUN WITH YOUR GREYHOUND

When your Greyhound becomes a settled member of the family, you may wish to expand your, and his, horizons and try some new challenges. Greyhounds and their owners are full of surprises, and a number of former racers have made their mark in different canine disciplines, ranging from Competitive Obedience, Agility, and Flyball to the rewarding work of training your Greyhound as a therapy dog, visiting the sick and elderly. Even if you do not have the time to take on a major training program, you can still have lots of fun with your Greyhound – and the more you do with your dog, the better your relationship will be.

CANINE GOOD CITIZEN

An excellent starting point is to enroll in the Canine Good Citizen scheme. This is a program for all dogs, regardless of age or breed, introduced by the Kennel Club (KC), in the UK, and the American Kennel Club (AKC). The aim is to raise awareness of responsible dog ownership and to instill basic good manners into the dogs taking part.

The Good Citizen scheme tests various aspects of a dog's behavior, assessing how well he has been socialized (e.g., whether he will accept being approached and petted by a stranger), and basic obedience (e.g., walking on the lead and responding to commands). The AKC states that the dog should be

- One that the judge would like to own
- One that would be safe with children
- One they would welcome as a neighbor
- One that makes his owner happy while not making someone else unhappy.

This may not be so taxing for a dog that has been reared and trained by his owner, but it is quite a test for the former racing Greyhound who has led such a different life.

The KC has three levels of difficulty (bronze, silver, and gold), and the AKC has just one test.

For full details of the scheme, contact your national kennel club.

PUBLIC RELATIONS AND FUND-RAISING

It is always a challenge to find homes for the many Greyhounds who become available each year. The adoption agencies work hard to publicize the fate of former racing dogs, but they are all desperately short of resources. In some cases, the public is unaware of the situation; in others, there is a prejudice against Greyhounds, born of a lack of knowledge and understanding.

The best way to counteract this prejudice is for the public to meet former racing dogs who have become companions. There are groups of Greyhound owners who meet together in parks to walk their dogs. They have literature from adoption agencies available for anyone who takes an interest. Their conversion rate has been spectacular!

Some adoption agencies will set up a trade stand at a country fair or a dog show to promote their work. Without exception, the stars of the show on these occasions are the retired Greyhounds, who cheerfully put up with being petted by hundreds of visitors. These public appearances not only help with finding new owners for former racers, but they also boost funds. There are many people who are not able to give a home to a Greyhound, but they are happy to give a donation or buy a raffle ticket.

Business and pleasure can be combined in the sponsored walks organized by some adoption agencies and owners' associations. Each dog and owner are sponsored by the mile, and everyone enjoys a great day out.

Fund-raising can be a great social event for both dogs and owners.

TOP AMBASSADOG

JoAnn Fotheringham first got involved with Greyhounds when she adopted Kayla. This beautiful black Greyhound changed her life, and she has gone on to dedicate most of her time and energy to raising money to rehome ex-racers.

"Kayla was a happy, energetic dog who loved to go on walks and be around people," said JoAnn. "She bonded with our family right away, and we felt that adoption was a wonderful experience. As the days went by, I just couldn't wait to get home from work to be with her. Our whole lives changed and revolved around Kayla. Wherever we were, people stopped to pet her and ask questions. She turned out to be quite an 'Ambassadog.' "

SETTING A GOAL

"Because of Kayla, I volunteered with Make Peace with Animals (a U.S. Greyhound rehoming agency), and I learned more about the breed. Since my children are grown, I had some free time on my hands, and what better way to use my time but to promote something I love – dogs, and especially Greyhounds. It was clear, Greyhound adoption was to be my goal."

JoAnn, who has adopted four Greyhounds in her own right, has now raised many thousands of dollars to help ex-racers. The fund-raising events she has been involved with include raffles, candy sales, bingo games, selling dog coats, plus other canine supplies and supplements. JoAnn also promotes the cause of ex-racers by promoting "meets and greets" at pet stores, organizing Greyhound parades, and attending school fairs and sporting events.

POT LUCK DINNER

The most unusual event she was involved with was a Greyhound Potluck Dinner, when families were invited to attend a supper, bringing their own food – and Greyhounds – with them. A total of 30 Greyhounds attended this mouth-watering event, and everyone had a great time. The Greyhounds were not excluded from the supper – they enjoyed special dog biscuits, made in the shape of hearts, to mark St. Valentine's day!

BETTER SHAPE

During the time JoAnn has been fund-raising for ex-racers, she has noticed a significant change in the dogs coming up for adoption. "In the past six years, I have seen a remarkable difference in the dogs coming off the track," she said. "They are in much better shape, coats are better, and some look like they just came out of a home. I feel that, if they are in that good shape just coming off the track, they must have been taken care of when they raced. The dogs love racing and enjoy being at the track. However, there is good and bad in every business or sport, so racing does have its share of bad that needs attention."

CALL FOR EDUCATION

In particular, JoAnn would like to see racing tracks setting aside funds to care for ex-racers, and financial help for staffing adoption kennels. She would also like to see the treatment of injured Greyhounds improved, so that a racing injury never precludes rehoming.

"Perhaps most important of all, I would like to see the public being educated about the Greyhounds that are available for adoption," said JoAnn. "Public service announcements could be made via television, radio, and magazines. This should be a worldwide campaign, and not just focused on the states or countries that have racing. We must keep lines of communication open and engender goodwill with the racing industry to be able to continue with the work we are doing."

ARTIFICIAL LURE COURSING

Coursing, which is on a strictly amateur basis, is far more prevalent in the United States. In the UK, it is better known among owners of other sighthounds. Before becoming involved, it is essential that your Greyhound is given a thorough check-over by a vet. It could well be that the dog has an underlying injury that was sustained during his racing days. This may be fine with gentle exercise, but serious damage could result if the dog attempts a more strenuous type of activity.

In the United States, two organizations hold coursing events – the American Sighthound Field Association (ASFA) and the American Kennel Club (AKC). In both organizations, the type of coursing is the same. The dogs, who include Greyhounds, Whippets, Salukis, Borzoi, Scottish Deerhounds, Irish Wolfhounds, Ibizan Hounds, Pharaoh Hounds, Afghans, Basenjis, and Rhodesian Ridgebacks, chase white plastic strips, attached to a string. This is threaded through a series of pulleys throughout the field, which creates a series of lefts and rights, a similar pattern to chasing live game.

The courses are a minimum of 600 yards, with 800–900 yards being the average. The dogs are judged on speed, agility, follow, and enthusiasm. The hounds run twice, in braces or in trios, and the scores are tallied at the end of the two runs.

Placements are determined in each breed by the combined scores of the preliminary and final runs. In the case of ties, the hounds are run off against each other to break the tie.

The other types of lure coursing include racing on a straight or an oval track, which is very similar to the type of racing seen at a professional Greyhound track. Amateur lure coursing is very much a family affair involving a wide mixture of people of all ages and all walks of life. The atmosphere is one of fun and camaraderie among novices and veterans alike. It is a very social activity, where many friendships are made – some of which may last a lifetime.

ON THE FAST TRACK

Tony and Cindy Scardaville, who are based in New Jersey, became involved in lure coursing purely by accident. They had adopted two former racing Greyhounds and went with their two dogs to get supplies at a local feed store. They were spotted by Mikey Stoble, a member of the local coursing club, and he invited them to come along to a club practice session.

"We thought it would make a good family outing so we went with our three sons," said Tony. "They were just about to release a Whippet for a run. Wow! In an instant, this hound was flying through the air chasing the white, plastic lure. The lure, through a system of pulleys, made a series of twists and turns, and all the while this little Whippet was hot on its trail. Finally, the lure returned to the starting point – and the smile on that dog's face was incredible! I looked at the rest of the family to see if they were as excited as I was, and they were...

"One of the club members asked if we would like to try our Greyhounds. First, they were

ON THE FAST TRACK

inspected for general condition, and we were asked questions about their health. We were given the go-ahead, and I brought our first Greyhound, our sweet, gentle Chela, to the line. I was shown how to hold the slip lead, and how to release her on the call of 'Tally ho.' The lure started to move, and I could feel the lead being strained and Chela was getting more and more excited. The signal was given, and Chela took off with a speed and an intensity that I had never seen before. She followed the lure with a determination that amazed me. From that moment, I realized that this was a sport I wanted to get involved with."

Tony now has nine sighthounds living with the family – five Greyhounds, two Salukis, and two Rampur Hounds – and he has become a well-known and respected figure on the coursing field. Between March and June and again between September and December, his dogs course once a week. His Greyhounds are all former racers, and he finds they need little additional training to be successful at coursing.

"The first order of business before starting coursing is to find out why a Greyhound has been retired, and/or to give him a thorough veterinary examination," he said. "This is to ensure that the hound does not have any previous serious injury which would prohibit him from running at speed again.

"The next step is to take the dog to lure coursing practices. Although the chase instinct has been reinforced with their track training, a racing Greyhound is only used to running in one direction, whereas, in coursing, the dogs have to make various types of turns. Former racers need to be introduced to this, but they usually learn the game fairly quickly."

Tony is often asked whether it can cause problems reawakening the chase instinct after a Greyhound has been retired from the track and is living, first and foremost, as a companion.

"The chase instinct is going to be there regardless of whether a Greyhound is allowed to course," he said. "The Greyhound has been bred for so many years to hunt and chase that the instinct is totally part of the breed. What coursing does do for a Greyhound is to make him a healthier, happier animal who gets to do something that comes naturally and that he enjoys."

Tony feeds all his dogs on a high-quality, meat-based kibble (complete food). The dogs' weight is monitored, and quantities adjusted to ensure that they maintain condition. The working dogs get kibble with a higher protein and fat content, and, just before an event, meat and supplements are given. This is to help rebuild muscle tissue after the rigors of running at speed.

"As far as exercise is concerned, I have a quarter of an acre which the hounds have free access to, allowing them to run and chase each

Pictured (left to right): Duke, Chela, and Lou, all great coursing enthusiasts.

ON THE FAST TRACK

Star: a natural on the coursing field.

other," said Tony. "I like them to run flat out once or twice a week, either during an organized practice or setting up my own equipment. This helps to ensure they maintain muscle tone and conditioning between meets."

Tony and his family have fostered many Greyhounds and are still very involved in helping to rehome former racers. There is one Greyhound that has a special place in his affections.

"We got Star, registered name E. F. Starchaser, as a foster animal who had bounced from a couple of homes," said Tony. "The problem was that Star had terrible sleep aggression, which was the result of some emotional trauma while he was still at the track. We would have to call him and wake him before entering a room where he was sleeping; otherwise, he would startle and jump up with all teeth bared. He meant no harm, but it could be quite intimidating for someone unfamiliar with this condition.

"It took us five months to help him get his confidence so that he stopped this behavior. By this time, we had become attached to him, and we were worried that, if he was adopted by someone else, he would have a relapse. We therefore decided to give him a permanent home.

"We were active members of the coursing club, so we took Star along to one of our practices. When he saw the lure move, he got very excited and it took everything I had to keep him restrained. I brought him to the line, and, on releasing him, I witnessed one of the most beautiful runs I have ever seen. Star was a natural! At the end of the course, his smile was so big I knew this was something I had to do with him.

"Star was in good condition, so it did not take much to get him into competition form. I switched him to the higher protein and fat diet that I give to all my working dogs, and started practicing with him every week. Shortly afterwards, I entered him in his first lure coursing trial where he proceeded to take first place. What a thrill! He continued to consistently place well and achieved a Field Champion title in short order. He is also titled in oval racing.

"Star retired from lure coursing when he was seven, due to a toe injury. Now aged 11, he continues to enjoy running about the yard. He is a real sweetheart and loves nothing better than to cuddle with me on the sofa whenever I sit down."

It was a real thrill to watch Star perform.

If you can establish a good level of control, your Greyhound will do well in Agility.

AGILITY

Agility has taken off in a big way since it was invented in the UK in the 1970s. It is based on an obstacle course against the clock, and both dogs and owners have to be fit to take part.

Again, you should make sure that your Greyhound has been checked by your vet before joining a club. Agility requires jumping and twisting as well as speed, so you must be confident that your dog is not likely to exacerbate an old injury.

The Agility course includes long and high jumps, tunnels, tires, weave poles, pause table, A-frame, see-saw, and an elevated plank called a dog-walk. It is tackled off-lead, with the handler giving directions.

Greyhounds certainly have the speed for this sport, and they can also be remarkably agile. In the UK, hurdles races are a popular feature at meetings, so clearly jumping comes naturally. Your main problem will probably be one of control. Your Greyhound must respond instantly to basic obedience commands – such as Sit, Stay, Down, and Come (see Chapter 6) – and you must be 100 percent sure that your Greyhound will return to you, regardless of distractions.

THERAPY DOGS

The importance of providing therapy with dogs is becoming increasingly widely recognized. For long-stay hospital patients, or for residents in homes for the elderly, life has little variety, and there is a feeling of isolation from the outside world.

Visits from therapy dogs have proved to be hugely beneficial, providing a topic for conversation, or just the comfort of stroking a loving and affectionate dog. Greyhounds, with their sweet, gentle temperament, are ideally suited to this work. Obviously, every dog must be checked for general good manners and soundness of temperament before beginning any therapy program.

THE GENTLE TOUCH

Kathy Bentzoni has two Greyhounds – CJ (CJ Monique) and O'Henry (BW's Red Rebel). She has trained both as therapy dogs and works with both children and adults.

"I think it is the Greyhound temperament which makes them so well suited to therapy work," said Kathy. "They are calm and gentle, and they are just the right height for visiting people who are in wheelchairs or in hospital beds.

"Before we started working, the dogs had to pass a special test. To begin with, they had to complete the American Kennel Club's Canine Good Citizen Test, and then they had to pass an additional test which exposed them to wheelchairs and canes, and to people handling them in different ways. The dogs also need to be able to Sit, Down, and Stay on command."

TALKING POINT

"I belong to a therapy dog group which organizes a range of different activities, mostly in nursing homes and hospitals. We go round to all the patients and ask if they would like to meet the dogs. It is really wonderful to see how these people light up when they see the dogs. Some even keep a special supply of biscuits for the dogs in anticipation of our visits.

"The dogs provide a topic of conversation and spark off old memories of previously owned pets. They also create a great feeling of warmth, and you can see the difference in the patients' demeanor from the minute we walk in."

KIDS' CAMP

"Every year, we make a special trip to a children's camp. This camp is organized for children who have lost their parents.

CJ and O'Henry have a special gentleness which makes them ideally suited to therapy work.

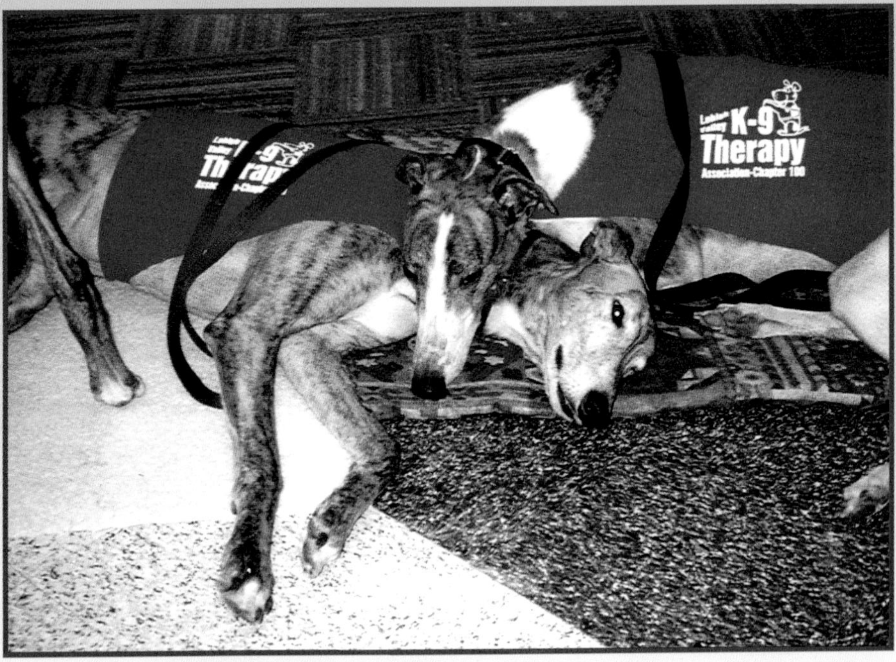

CJ and O'Henry taking a well-deserved break.

"We go along on the first night, and the children are told how the Greyhounds are starting a new life after they have finished their racing careers.

"This ties in with the message of renewal and regrowth for children who are having to come to terms with big changes in their own lives. It is often very moving.

"We have a question-and-answer session, and then the kids get to interact with the dogs, hugging them and petting them. I always leave the camp with a huge feeling of respect for the special bond that exists between dogs and humans."

CHAPTER EIGHT

HEALTH CARE

By John Kohnke BVSc RDA

Greyhounds are a responsive, intelligent, adaptable, and easily-cared-for short-haired breed of dog. Once retired from racing, they are well mannered and obedient, becoming loving companion animals. They suffer from very few inherent problems, but a small minority may carry a legacy of injury from the race track into retirement.

Greyhounds are relatively large dogs that require space to live and exercise. Unfortunately, once settled into a sedentary lifestyle as a family pet, they are prone to obesity if they are fed excessive food or high-calorie diets, or if they lack the opportunity to exercise on the lead or free-run on a regular basis.

Your retired Greyhound can be expected to live to an age of 12 to 14 years, which is a good life expectancy for a large breed of dog. Obviously, this will depend on the animal's individual health, housing, the type and extent of injury on retirement, and how well the diet and exercise program is managed.

This chapter provides guidelines for general health care and feeding, and outlines some of the more common problems that can affect retired racers and rescued Greyhounds as they age.

GENERAL HEALTH CARE

Greyhounds average from 57 lb (26 kg) for small bitches to 79 lb (36 kg) for larger framed dogs in race training in athletic, lean condition. On retirement, they can be expected to gain from 4.4 to 8.8 lb (2 to 4 kg) in weight without bordering on obesity. You should assess your newly adopted Greyhound's general condition and, if necessary, have the animal checked over by your vet.

Luckily, many Greyhounds are retired from racing because they are not competitive, lack speed, or are not trained to their full genetic potential. Others are retired because of injury,

Your veterinarian will advise on a program of vaccination.

most commonly to muscles, bones, joints, or toes. These dogs may have scars, swellings, enlarged joints, missing toes, and varying degrees of joint discomfort and arthritis.

It is a good idea to be forewarned on the likelihood of long-term degenerative conditions, such as osteoarthritic joint problems, so that you can take preventive measures as early as possible to give your Greyhound the best chance of living an active and long life.

VACCINATION

Although your retired Greyhound will have had the mandatory primary course of vaccinations against common viral diseases that affect all breeds of dogs, it is important that you arrange regular booster shots, starting as soon as the Greyhound enters his well-earned retirement (assuming it has been a year since he was last vaccinated). Your vet will be able to advise on the types of vaccination required in your area, but generally a full cover against all common diseases provides the best long-term protection and state of health. If you do not have a vaccination history, then the best policy is to revaccinate the Greyhound on arrival at your home.

The major viral diseases are canine distemper, canine hepatitis (adenovirus), canine parvovirus, viral rabies, and, from time to time, canine herpes virus, canine coronavirus, and canine para-influenza virus. Occasionally, Leptospira spp. bacterial infections, and, in the United States, Lyme disease, caused by a bacterial organism, will infect local dog populations.

Often, canine viruses have a cyclical nature of outbreaks as vaccination frequency and, therefore, immune protection wanes in dog populations. Taking your Greyhound out for exercise on the street or along the roadside, in the park or to a show competition can expose the animal to viral infections passed on by infected or carrier dogs. Often, stray, uncared-for dogs that roam public places searching for food or shelter harbor and spread distemper to other dogs that are exposed to viruses shed from carrier animals. Infected animals can spread the common viruses by nasal (aerosol) droplets (e.g., distemper, hepatitis) or shed the viruses in their droppings, including distemper, hepatitis, canine coronavirus, or parvovirus.

The common respiratory disease, infectious tracheitis or "kennel cough," usually infects young or aged dogs, causing a persistent rasping cough. In some countries, combined infection with viral para-influenza and bacterial Bordatella organisms produces the characteristic symptoms, with natural or vaccine immunity only lasting for six to eight months. This disease, although not life-threatening, is most commonly spread by carrier animals at shows or where dogs are in close contact, such as in boarding kennels or obedience training classes. If your Greyhound is at risk for these reasons, then it is best to maintain a program of regular vaccinations.

Annual booster vaccinations against common or "core" diseases in each country are still considered to be the most effective means of maintaining strong immunity against potentially life-threatening diseases. These include canine distemper that causes long-term nerve damage; canine parvovirus that can weaken the heart or damage the gut lining; canine adenovirus that results in hepatitis and a risk of long-term liver failure; and "zoonotic" diseases such as rabies, a nervous disease that can be fatal in humans.

Your own vet will advise you on the most suitable vaccination program that will protect your Greyhound and other dogs. Ask to be sent an annual booster reminder card to ensure that you take your Greyhound for regular vaccinations. Remember that vaccination is the simple, most effective method of preventing common diseases, which can be expensive to treat or even fatal. Modern vaccines have very little risk of side effects or other adverse reactions, if administered as recommended.

There is effective treatment for all internal parasites.

INTERNAL PARASITES

An effective regular worming program is the best way to keep your Greyhound as worm-free as possible. It is true to say that most dogs have some worms, simply because the most common types are spread by worm eggs passed in the stools. Dog droppings contaminate the kennel area, outside lawns, yards, and parkland exercise areas. Some worm eggs can be carried and spread by water after rainfall.

Internal parasites use the dog's bowels or body for nutrition, warmth, and lodging, without contributing to well-being or health. They cause varying degrees of internal bowel and organ damage; they can suck blood or, in the case of heartworm, obstruct the heart chambers and cause secondary vascular and lung conditions as a Greyhound ages.

If you have young children, it is especially important to treat your Greyhound for roundworm infestation.

Roundworms

Greyhounds can harbor two species of roundworm, the most common being *Toxocara canis*. This is a white worm that can develop to the thickness of spaghetti and measures from 3 to 6 inches (7 to 15 cm) in length. Almost all puppies are at risk, as they are infected through the womb, or via the milk or teats as they suckle. Heavy burdens compete for nutrients, causing poor growth as well as diarrhea and vomiting. The sheer volume of worms in the small bowel can result in bowel obstruction, or a characteristic "pot-bellied" appearance, with poor overall condition in a puppy up to three to four months of age.

By 9 to 12 months of age, growing dogs develop active immunity against roundworm infection, with studies indicating that only about 12 percent of adult Greyhounds pass roundworm eggs in their stools. Although older or sick dogs can develop heavy burdens because of waning immunity, few show symptoms. Unfortunately, roundworms can be transmitted via eggs from dogs to humans, especially children who lack immune defense.

It is therefore important to treat your retired Greyhound regularly for roundworms, especially if young children touch or stroke the animal or crawl on floors or grass that may become contaminated with infective eggs. Everyone should get into the habit of washing their hands after contact with the dog, especially children.

Hookworms

Hookworms are most common in Greyhounds that are kept in damp outside runs or those that visit parkland where other dogs congregate. Two species of hookworm occur in dogs, with the prevalence varying from country to country. The *Uncinaria* species is the most prevalent in colder countries, and the *Ancylostomum* species occurs in moderate to warm countries. The *Ancylostomum* species sucks blood from the bowel wall and even relatively small worm burdens can cause anemia, pale gums, and a dry, dull coat. With heavy burdens, there may also be a loss of stamina and condition. The *Uncinaria* species gnaw on the gut wall, causing irritation, blood loss and reduced nutrient uptake, poor condition, and a dull, rough coat.

Hookworm larvae, hatching from eggs, are passed in the stools of infected dogs and can move along the kennel floor, bedding, ground, or grass surface. The larvae re-infect by penetrating the skin on the webbing of the feet of the Greyhound, or other areas of contact with the ground. They can also be taken in with spilt food or bones eaten on the floor. Damp, low spots, where water collects in a yard, provide ideal conditions for reservoirs of infective hookworm larvae.

The larvae can also penetrate the soles of the feet of children or adults standing barefooted in a contaminated area, causing uncomfortable irritation and itching. The infective larvae can even emerge to the surface from buried droppings in the garden or the dog's run, even through 6 inches (15 cm) of damp soil. Hygienic disposal of droppings, away from living or exercise areas, is an important part of worm control in all dogs.

Tapeworms

Adult Greyhounds can become infected with a number of species of tapeworm or flatworms, called cestodes. Even heavy burdens of tapeworms cause few health effects in mature Greyhounds. Certain species of tapeworm eggs can also develop in humans as an intermediate host, causing serious organ damage, which may be fatal. Tapeworms are not directly spread from dog to dog via eggs, but the eggs are first ingested by an intermediate host, and then they develop into an infective stage. They are then taken back into the dog when the intermediate host is eaten.

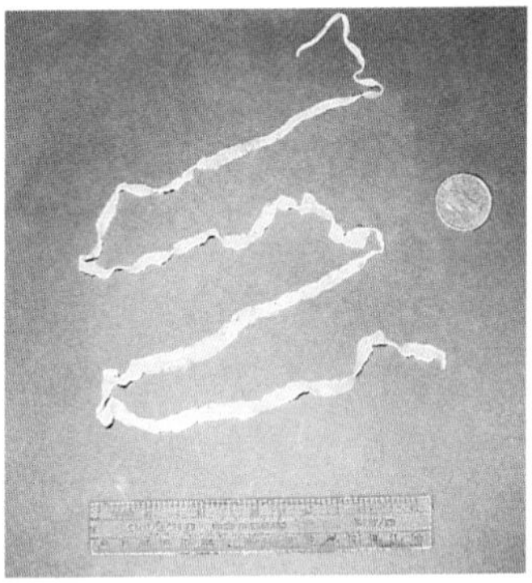

Tapeworm passed by an adult dog. (The coin gives an indication of size.)

Greyhounds confined to outside runs may be at risk from whipworms.

Rats, mice, and the common dog flea can act as common intermediate hosts in a Greyhound's kennel environment, with the most common tapeworm, *Dipylidium caninum*, being carried by fleas. Infective fleas are gnawed off and eaten by dogs as they bite flea-ridden itchy areas, completing the life cycle to enable mature tapeworms to develop in the dog's bowel.

Dipylidium caninum can develop into a segmented, large worm up to 18 inches (50 cm) in length. The segments of the tapeworm carrying the eggs break off in the bowels, being shed into the stools as white, moving objects similar in size and appearance to cucumber seeds or flattened rice grains. They can also be seen as they crawl around the dog's anal area, escaping from stools retained in the animal's rectum. Signs of infection include skidding the backside along carpet or grass to relieve the "tickling" sensation as the segments move around the anal area, as well as visible segments moving on the dog's stools. Treatment by regular worming, combined with rigorous flea control, will help keep your retired Greyhound free from the most common tapeworm.

Ensuring that your Greyhound is provided with only abattoir-inspected raw lamb and mutton meat, or liver, beef, pork, or horsemeat, and denying him the opportunity to scavenge carcasses, will help reduce the chance of the animal carrying tapeworms which could be transmitted to humans. Controlling rats and mice in outside kennels is also an important control measure.

Whipworms

Whipworms, or the *Trichuris* species, of which two types can infect Greyhounds, are long, thin worms that colonize the large bowel of dogs, causing gut discomfort and irritation, mucus- or blood-smeared stools, and anemia in heavy burdens. Greyhounds confined to outside runs are most at risk because viable whipworm eggs can survive in soil surface debris for years. Regular worming with strict kennel and yard hygiene to pick up droppings will effectively control whipworms.

The mosquito is a carrier of heartworm.

Lung or "Windpipe" Worms

Young Greyhounds in race training have a reasonable risk of becoming infected with a thin, thread-like worm, *Filaroides osleri*, with up to 18 percent of racing Greyhounds carrying burdens in two UK surveys. The adult worms colonize the lower windpipe area, living in nodules, with eggs being coughed up in mucus. This can be observed as a characteristic "rasping" type of cough during or following exercise, as the eggs are swallowed and passed out in the stools. Unfortunately, control of lung worms by standard worming compounds is not very effective, and, if you are alerted by a rasping, throaty type of cough, particularly after exercising your Greyhound, have the animal checked by your vet for tracheal worms.

Heartworm

Greyhounds living in the United States and northern and eastern Australia have a high risk of developing an infestation of the canine heartworm, *Dirofilaria immitis*, a long, thin worm that colonizes the right-side chambers of the heart. The worm is spread by microscopic larvae (called microfilariae), which are taken in by female mosquitoes in a blood meal when they bite the infected dog carrying adult heartworms. After a period of three weeks, infective stages can be transmitted by the roaming mosquito back into dogs. Adult heartworms develop six months later in the heart.

In areas where heartworm is common and preventative treatments with specific drugs are not given or rigorously maintained, heartworm disease is the most common cause of heart problems in older, retired Greyhounds.

Heartworms can develop to 12 inches (30 cm) in length, and large numbers of these thread-like worms can obstruct the right-side heart chambers, causing severe blood-flow impairment to the lungs. This results in a moist type of cough, usually at night when the Greyhound is resting, as fluid accumulates in the lungs. The Greyhound often develops a characteristic premature graying of the muzzle and face, and coughs and attempts to vomit or "gag" to remove excess fluid in his throat. The animal characteristically lacks stamina and tires easily when exercising. Mature heartworms can be removed by special arsenic-type drugs, with, however, a risk of toxic reaction or death.

A strict program of administering daily or monthly preventative oral medication, controlling mosquitoes, or keeping your Greyhound inside from before sunset until after dawn when mosquitoes are most prevalent will help reduce the risk of this type of heartworm. In the United States, many vets recommend year-round preventive treatment, although some owners prefer to restrict treatment to the mosquito months (May to November). Another smaller species of heartworm, *Dipetalonema reconditum,* is spread by fleas, but even heavy burdens do not appear to cause severe health problems.

Control of Internal Parasites

Your vet can provide you with the most effective treatment program and advice on specific worming compounds to ensure that your retired Greyhound is kept as worm-free as possible. It is also essential to maintain strict hygiene by promptly removing droppings from the kennel area, from lawn areas surrounding the house, or from outside runs. Regular treatment for fleas is an important measure to keep the common tapeworm under control. Secondary preventative measures for tapeworm include avoiding feeding noninspected raw, red meat and controlling rats and mice. Mosquitoes should be controlled in areas where canine heartworm is endemic.

EXTERNAL PARASITES

Greyhounds are hosts to fleas and occasionally lice. When Greyhounds are exercised in fields or woodland areas in late summer and autumn, they may also be exposed to ticks and grass or harvest mites.

Fleas

Fleas are by far the most common external parasite, and although Greyhounds have a short-haired coat, fleas can be a year-round problem when dogs are kept indoors or under warm conditions, if adequate and regular flea control measures are not adopted. Fleas need a meal of

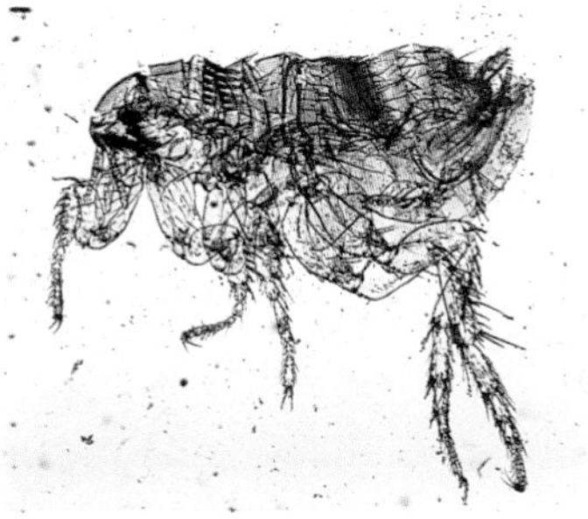

The dog flea – Ctenocephalides canis.

blood to complete their breeding and egg-laying life cycle. Eggs hatch in the environment into small moving larvae that are attracted to any warm mammalian body, including those of dogs, cats, rodents, or humans.

Although some Greyhounds can carry heavy infestations of dog fleas, cat fleas, or even hedgehog fleas, without any obvious annoyance or skin problem, other Greyhounds can develop an acute allergic skin condition after being bitten by only one or two fleas.

A flea can bite a dog up to 600 times per day to suck blood, depositing small amounts of saliva within the skin. The "foreign" saliva may initiate a highly allergic dermatitis reaction, leading to scratching, gnawing, and matting of the hair and attracting more fleas to the traumatized, lacerated, and bleeding skin. Fleas tend to congregate on the rear underbelly area, over the rear of the hindquarters and around the tail butt area, where a dog cannot effectively scratch. However, dogs will bite and gnaw these areas, softening the skin and intensifying the cycle of allergic reaction.

Sensitive Greyhounds will often attempt to rub the itchy area on furniture to relieve the itch, depositing skin debris and blood fluid that stains and fouls the surface.

Fleas most commonly lay eggs in the dog's bedding, in cracks in wooden floors, in carpets, or in the debris of grass in outside runs. Adult fleas can survive in the environment for up to 12 months without feeding and can jump up to 3 feet (1 meter) to hitch a ride and a feed on a dog. Thus, reservoirs of fleas can survive in carpets, bedding, and surface debris in yards, for 6 to 12 months, often between summer seasons in warmer environments.

Control of fleas must combine regular fortnightly flea washes with the combing-in of flea powders, especially during the warmer months, or with the use of insecticides applied to the coat or the skin in the form of a spot-on treatment or a spray. Some of these treatments will kill fleas for up to three months. Oral flea treatments, given daily or twice weekly with food, are available in some countries, and should

A spray-on flea treatment is an effective measure to take.

be used in conjunction with a program of environmental control. A thorough vacuuming of infested carpets will vibrate flea eggs, causing them to hatch. The developing fleas can be killed by a follow-up insecticide treatment four to seven days later. The Greyhound's bedding and mats on favorite napping or resting areas should be changed regularly or treated with insecticidal washes. Other dogs in the household should be treated, and their bedding should be changed at the same time.

Lice

Lice infestation is not common in Greyhounds because they have a short coat that does not protect lice from cold conditions. Lice are transmitted from dog to dog by contact and can only survive off a dog for a short time. The life cycle of lice is completed entirely on the dog, with small, grayish, oval-shaped eggs or "nits" attached to the hairs.

Even a light infestation of lice can cause a Greyhound to scratch, bite, and rub the itchy areas. Bathing the animal twice with an insecticidal shampoo formulated for dogs, 14 days apart, will break the life cycle. This should be combined with a preparation to relieve the itch if necessary, and with the treatment of bedding or mats, which lice may have established as a reservoir of re-infestation.

Ticks

There are a number of ticks that live primarily in the outdoor environment and on other host animals. These ticks can colonize Greyhounds. Ticks are usually visible on a short-haired, sleek Greyhound because of their larger size and characteristic enlargement as they attach to suck blood. Ticks can be carried on hedgehogs, sheep, and other warm-blooded animals in woodland areas. In America, certain species of ticks can carry a bacterial organism that causes Lyme disease, a fatal nervous disease in dogs. It has also been discovered that some 30 percent of American dogs test positive for tick-borne diseases such as Ehrlichia, Rocky Mountain Fever, and Babesia, which can prove fatal if they are not treated.

On the eastern coastline of Australia, the tick *Ixodes holocyclus* is carried by bandicoots and can attach to a dog. As it sucks blood, the tick secretes a powerful paralysis chemical into the animal, which, if not recognized and removed, is invariably fatal.

Bedding should be treated with an insecticidal wash.

Check your dog for ticks if you have been walking in long grass.

After each walk in long grass, a careful examination of your Greyhound should be carried out to check for ticks attached to the skin on the sides or underbelly, including in the ears and under the tail and webbing of the feet. This should be adopted as a routine control measure in known tick-infested areas. Again, use of insecticidal shampoos is recommended if ticks are a local or seasonal problem. Some shampoos and insecticide washes provide residual activity against ticks for three to four weeks.

Mites

Greyhounds, as they age, can develop the characteristic patches of hair loss associated with the skin or mange mite, Demodectes, and, occasionally, infection with Sarcoptes mange mites. Demodectic mange is caused by a small mite that burrows into the hair follicles, causing an immune reaction that can suppress their activity and lead to the development of mange or hair loss on the muzzle and around the eyes, face, and front limbs. Demodectic mange mites can be passed by a bitch to her puppies and remain dormant in the skin as immunity develops against the mites.

As Greyhounds grow older, or suffer from ill health, the immune suppression is reduced, allowing the mites to become more active, leading to symptoms of mange. (See skin conditions, page 122.)

Occasionally, a Greyhound taken for a walk in long grass on a farm or rural roadside can pick up skin mites. These mites are usually small white "dandruff" mites or red "harvest" mites that can be seen with a magnifying glass on the head and chest and between the back legs and lower limbs. The dog will usually develop an intense itching and scratching, without signs of fleas, within a short time after a walk in an infected area. Washing the dog in an insecticidal shampoo or spray usually controls the mites effectively. Repeat treatments may have to be carried out if the animal is walked in the infested area again, so it is best to avoid known mite havens.

A species of Otodectes mites can also colonize

the ear canal, causing irritation and scratching in the ears. (See ear conditions, page 120.)

TEETH CARE

Regular teeth and gum care is important in all Greyhounds, especially if you feed soft, mushy foods that build up a residue between the teeth. In common with other breeds of dogs, Greyhounds often gnaw or lick themselves, which introduces a higher bacterial load into the mouth cavity, resulting in gum infection and laceration from strands of hair caught between the teeth.

Often the teeth of a Greyhound in a training kennel become coated with tartar or plaque with development of a reddened tooth-gum infection or gingivitis. In severe cases, this causes the gums to bleed and create foul breath (halitosis) as the accumulation of bacteria ferment carbohydrate and protein residues, producing acids that erode the tooth enamel and start the decay process.

High bacterial loads harbored in the mouth from gnawing the skin and licking the genital areas can cause tonsilitis, with loss of appetite due to sore, inflamed throat tonsils. The front teeth can also be worn down to the gum margins if a Greyhound eats from a hard ceramic food bowl.

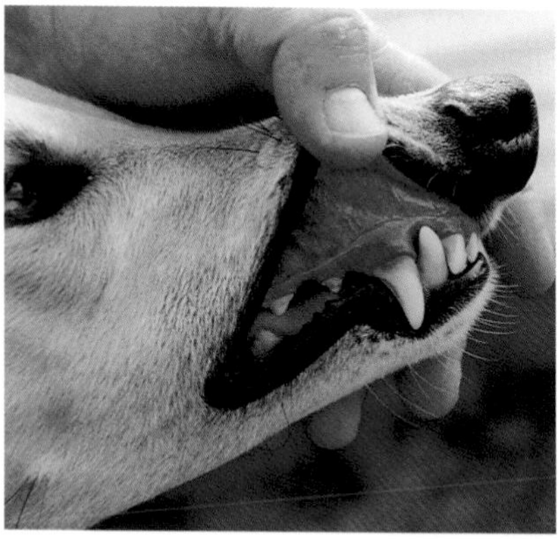

Tartar will accumulate on the teeth, particularly as the Greyhound gets older.

Greyhounds have a long nasal and mouth jawline, which allows easy access to most of the teeth to check for tartar and trapped food residues. If a heavy accumulation of tartar is present as a yellowish-brown crust-like covering on the gum margins of the large canine teeth or molar teeth, then it is best to have the teeth descaled by your vet. You can then check the teeth regularly yourself for buildup of plaque or tartar.

Toothpastes for dogs are available, but regular daily use is a must to keep the teeth clean. Providing an 8-ounce (250-g) piece of spongy beef brisket bone (in BSE-free countries) or rib for the animal to gnaw regularly once a week (under supervision) helps to keep teeth clean and massages the gums to keep them healthy. Hard rusks, and dry foods containing a chemical called sodium hexametaphosphate as an antiplaque coating, are also useful. However, if the tooth-gum margins become inflamed or reddened, or the Greyhound develops halitosis, then use a cotton swab to apply a solution of 50:50 hydrogen peroxide and bicarb solution to the gum margin areas. This will "fizz" and oxygenate the gaps between the teeth. Continue the treatment for four to five days to discourage bacterial buildup and to sweeten the breath, as well as restore the teeth to a clean, white appearance.

As your Greyhound ages, regular teeth care becomes even more important. Older

Greyhounds may have decayed molar teeth that can break or split when chewing on bones. If teeth split, break, or decay away, symptoms of toothache and toxic infection with inflamed gums and lymph nodes (almond-sized lumps) between the bottom jaws can develop, leading to an uncharacteristic reluctance to eat or obvious pain and discomfort. A visit to your vet may be necessary for descaling, filling to repair decayed areas, or extraction of diseased teeth.

Providing your Greyhound with a soft plastic bowl or aluminum dish (with a ceramic tile glued to the underneath to prevent it from being tipped over) is helpful to reduce undue wear and erosion of the front teeth. If your aged Greyhound has poor teeth, then soft, complete foods that require minimal chewing are useful to ensure that the animal obtains maximum benefit from his food. Canned dog food and biscuits that are soaked with water, or diluted with meat stock or broth to a "mushy" but not excessively soft consistency, can be fed. Bones that can be crushed by the weakened molar (jaw) teeth should be avoided, as they may lead to broken teeth and impaction of the hind bowel in older dogs.

Greyhounds have very good eyesight.

EYES

Greyhounds are sighthounds and have very prominent eyeballs and good vision. Eye conditions are not common, but they can occur over various areas of the eye, restricting a Greyhound's vision. On rare occasions in race training, particles of sand flicked into the eyes from the track can lacerate, infect, and scar the cornea, which can be seen as a white area on the clear part of the eyeball. Severe lacerations can affect the animal's vision, but Greyhounds adjust to impaired vision well and can enjoy relatively normal lifestyles.

Another condition, referred to as "pannus" or Superficial Stromal Keratitis (SSK), is considered to be an auto-immune-triggered reaction to ultraviolet light and can cause clouding of the cornea, with a web-like growth of blood vessels and an appearance of deposits and dark pigment that slowly spreads across the cornea. The eye often weeps and is held partly closed due to the irritation, pain, and associated photophobia (sensitivity to light). Treatment by your vet with long-acting corticosteroid preparations can help to control the condition to allow your Greyhound to lead a sight-restricted, but otherwise normal, life. Ensuring that the Greyhound has access to a shaded area is recommended, to avoid unnecessary exposure to bright sunlight and ultraviolet rays.

Greyhounds can also develop a genetic form of progressive retinal atrophy, resulting in a slow deterioration of the light-sensitive membrane on the inside rear of the eyeball. This is referred to as central progressive retinal atrophy. A progressive loss of sight occurs, leading to daylight blindness. The eyes appear as bright-green glowing circles if a flashlight is directed into the dilated pupils. Unfortunately, there is no treatment, and eventually the Greyhound becomes sight-impaired. Greyhounds may be retired early from racing because of poor vision in night races.

As Greyhounds age, in common with most dogs, they are likely to develop cataracts, which appear as an opaque "crystallization" of the lens behind the pupil. Usually a cataract develops initially in one eye but will eventually affect both eyes with the characteristic dilated pupils and "glistening" lens.

Most Greyhounds can cope with progressive blindness as their sight becomes dimmer, and, provided they are kept in familiar surroundings, they can remain active and able to find their way around by memory, smell, and sound. Surgery to remove the affected lens and replace it with a prosthetic lens is now widely carried out to correct cataracts in aged dogs.

Some Greyhounds' ears will go fully erect when a sound catches their attention.

EARS

Greyhounds have erect ears that often turn over to the front when relaxed, becoming more directed when using their eyes to observe moving objects in the far distance. The combination of erect ears and wide ear canals improves drainage of the ears, which helps to reduce the risk of Greyhounds developing ear canal infections. However, ear mite infection, with Otodectes species, can occasionally develop in older Greyhounds, although it is most common in young animals, often causing inflammation and a smelly discharge from the ear canal. Many older Greyhounds can harbor the small white mites within their ear canal, without any outward signs. Ear mites can survive away from a dog for several weeks and can hide in the hair covering the face, neck, and feet, migrating to the head to re-infect the ears.

As a Greyhound ages in retirement or develops a chronic illness, his immunity may wane, which can result in ear mites building up in the warm, waxy, and moist ear canal, irritating the lining tissue. Secondary bacterial, fungal, or yeast cell infections can establish as a result of this irritation of the ear canal. A smelly, dark discharge can develop, commonly referred to as canker (otitis externa). Canker is particularly common in water dogs with long, pendulous ears and tortuous ear canals. Treatment supervised by your vet, with dewaxing and soothing miticide drops, will usually clear up ear mite infection. This, combined with a weekly body wash with an insecticidal shampoo, as well as treatment of the bedding and favorite resting areas, will usually break the life cycle.

Two other common problems can develop on the tips and edges of a Greyhound's ears, one during cold winter months and the other during the warmer months.

Chilblains cause drying and painful cracking of the tips of the ears under cold conditions. Greyhounds have thin ears with little insulating hair and small blood vessels close to the skin. Chilblains are a mild stage of frostbite and are a major problem in cold, wintry conditions when Greyhounds are walked or housed outdoors.

When the Greyhound is relaxed, his ears will fold.

The skin on the borders of the ears becomes devitalized and develops moist areas of necrotic tissue. Rubbing the sore ears exacerbates the weeping sores, often causing the edges to ulcerate, seep blood, and attract flies. In early cases, warm ferments will assist circulation, with healing promoted by soothing creams and antibiotics. However, the ears must be protected from the cold, by either pinning them against the head with a band of woolen, stretchy football sock or with a sleeve of a cardigan. Your Greyhound will relish being housed indoors in a heated room during cold weather for comfort and to avoid chilblains.

During the warmer months of the year, flies, mosquitoes, and biting insects can cause irritation to the ear tips and edges of a Greyhound's ear flap.

Under swarming conditions, these insects bite the exposed, thinly covered skin on the ear flap edges, resulting in scabby, moist skin and matting of the surrounding hair, which then attracts even more flies. The Greyhound can exacerbate the trauma by rubbing the ears with the front paws, shaking, or scratching. Application of soothing insect repellent lotions each morning and evening, combined with drying preparations overnight, can help to reduce insect annoyance.

Some Greyhounds may develop skin conditions when they move into a home environment.

Covering the ears with gauze or the feet pockets of pantyhose may also protect the ears of sensitive Greyhounds as they reach their senior years.

SKIN CONDITIONS

Greyhounds characteristically suffer from few skin problems, such as dermatitis or eczema, if they are housed under clean, dry conditions and brushed regularly. The majority of skin problems are initiated by fleas or insects. However, some Greyhounds can develop allergies to certain foods, which are manifested by skin allergy reactions, inflammation, or dermatitis, with itching and occasionally increased shedding of skin cells or "scurf," similar to human dandruff.

Dandruff is most noticeable on black-coated Greyhounds as small whitish skin flakes. Some Greyhounds scratch the front half of their bodies or lick, bite, or gnaw themselves on the hind areas to relieve itches and irritation, leading to a degree of self-mutilation of the head, neck, underbelly, feet, and tail butt area.

An atopic dermatitis may develop on some Greyhounds, initiated by an antibody reaction to allergens contained in foods or food preservatives, by dust mites and their droppings in house carpets, or by an allergy to carpets or bedding.

Skin conditions are more likely in retired Greyhounds living indoors. Contact with shampoo or soap residues can irritate and cause dermatitis in sensitive, thin-skinned Greyhounds. The webbing of the feet may become inflamed and itchy following contact with newly cut grass, chemical cleaners, or pool chlorine residues.

If the skin allergy becomes severe or recurring, then diagnosis and treatment by your vet is recommended. If an atopic dermatitis is suspected, then progressive elimination of foods from the diet can be of help in identifying a food allergy. A change in the type of bedding or coat shampoo may help to reduce the skin reaction.

Dietary supplements of essential fatty acids, often based on evening primrose oil with gamma linoleic acid (GLA), trace minerals, and vitamins, may help to prevent atopic allergies and "dandruff" in the coat of Greyhounds as they age.

Mange, which is most commonly caused by the burrowing skin mite *Demodex canis*, can develop in retired Greyhounds as their immunity wanes due to sickness, stress, or old age. The mites can colonize the skin glands and hair follicles in puppyhood, particularly around the muzzle, face, and front limbs.

They often remain dormant for years due to the buildup of immunity, which suppresses mite numbers and activity in a healthy Greyhound. Hair loss on the muzzle and around the eyes and front limbs combined with a moist, greasy skin surface and "rancid fat" odor (due to secondary bacterial or fungal infection) are telltale signs of demodectic mange in older Greyhounds. Diagnosis can be confirmed by skin scrapings taken by your vet.

Infection with another mange mite, the Sarcoptic mite, can also cause intense irritation, itching, and scratching, as the mites burrow into the skin to feed, develop, and lay eggs, often in localized areas of thin skin such as the chest, belly, elbows, and borders of the ears. The affected ears often become infected with bacteria as the Greyhound licks and scratches the skin, resulting in a greasy, oily, and smelly surface covered with crusty scabs. The mites are usually introduced by an already-infected dog and can only live off the Greyhound for two or three days. Greyhounds with sarcoptic mange can transfer the mites to human handlers, causing an itchy dermatitis on the elbows and armpits.

Treatment with insecticidal washes over a four- to six-week period, combined with antibiotics to control skin infection, will assist in the control of the mites and restore skin health, complemented by supplements of essential oils and vitamins A and E. All dogs in the household should be treated at the same time, and their bedding should be washed and changed.

DIGESTIVE PROBLEMS

Feeding a hygienically prepared, well-balanced diet and maintaining a clean, regularly sanitized living area will help to minimize digestive upset in your Greyhound. Greyhounds that are allowed to roam freely are likely to consume contaminated or rotting food or scraps, which will ultimately lead to gastro-intestinal irritation and infection, with loose bowels or smelly diarrhea.

However, some Greyhounds can develop individual intolerances to certain foods, such as raw red meats, soya-bean-based dry foods, or excessive amounts of milk in their diets. These intolerances can predispose them to low-grade, recurring diarrhea. Certain Greyhounds, if given unlimited access to dry foods, may overeat and develop loose bowels and, in time, obesity.

As they age, the digestive efficiency often decreases, leading to reduced food absorption and loose bowels, which can be exacerbated by particular types of intestinal cancers.

If your Greyhound develops a fever, gut discomfort, and dehydration or passes blood in his stools as a result of a sudden bout of diarrhea, diagnosis by your vet is recommended. Antibiotics and fluid therapy may be required, combined with nursing and rest.

Other forms of diarrhea often settle down by limiting food intake for 24 to 48 hours to rest the gut and by providing rehydration fluids to restore body fluids. Often, a course of a probiotic supplement containing *Lactobacilli acidophilus* and other digestive bacteria is also useful.

Older retired Greyhounds can also develop impaction of the intestines if given bones to gnaw to clean their teeth. Bones that have been cooked in meat should not be given at any time because they are likely to shatter into sharp fragments when crushed by the teeth, causing lacerations to the mouth and bowels, as well as impaction.

Greyhounds are more likely to suffer increasing frequency of impacted large intestines as they age, especially if fed on a dry-food diet without adequate moisture, or if they do not drink enough water under cool conditions. Signs include straining and difficulty in passing dry, crumbly stools. In serious cases, severe constipation and discomfort will require veterinary treatment.

Feeding a laxative diet with moistened dry food, up to one cup of cooked vegetables daily for fiber (or two tablespoons of bran flakes), and limiting access to larger pieces of bone, or denying bones to an aged Greyhound with poor teeth, will help reduce bowel impaction.

Many older dogs also develop impacted anal glands, the two small scent-secreting glands within their anal ring. Feeding a soft diet that does not "massage" the anal glands as the stools are passed or confining a Greyhound inside can result in prolonged fecal retention in the rectum, leading to infection of the anal glands.

The Greyhound will attempt to relieve the discomfort by scraping or skidding his backside along a grassy area, or on house carpets. These

Feeding a well-balanced diet will help to prevent many digestive problems.

Gnawing a bone can help digestion as well as keep the teeth clean.

are also signs consistent with infection with the common tapeworm (see page 111), as the moving segments tickle the anal area. Occasionally, a severely impacted and infected anal gland will burst through the anal ring, exuding a pungent, foul-smelling, creamy discharge onto carpets and the living area.

Feeding a 10.5-oz (300-gram) soft, spongy portion of brisket bone once weekly will help to clean the teeth as the bone is gnawed and increase fecal consolidation to squeeze the anal glands as stools are passed.

However, bones are likely to cause fecal impaction in aged Greyhounds, so careful monitoring for signs of anal gland irritation and regular expressing of the glands by your vet is the best way to prevent discomfort and smelly anal discharges. Your vet may demonstrate the technique to express the anal glands if a Greyhound has recurring problems. Removal of the glands by surgery is another option in an older Greyhound plagued by the condition.

DIABETES

Greyhounds, like other breeds of dogs, are prone to developing "sugar" diabetes as they age. It is referred to as Diabetes mellitus, distinct from Diabetes insipidus, colloquially termed "racing thirst" or "water" diabetes that can affect racing Greyhounds as a result of extreme physical stress.

Many older Greyhounds may start to urinate in the house when confined indoors overnight. This may progress to dribbling weak, colorless urine when walked on the lead. Affected Greyhounds start to drink more water, become less active, lose weight, and become dehydrated and "tucked up" in the belly. This common form of diabetes is caused by decreased insulin secretion from the pancreas gland, as in older humans; bloodline susceptibility is not considered common in Greyhounds.

The elevated levels of blood sugar result in overflow of glucose through the kidneys and subsequent increased urine output, which tests positive for glucose. If not recognized and treated with daily doses of insulin under veterinary supervision, affected aged Greyhounds may develop muscle weakness and collapse during a diabetic coma. Reduction of starch and soluble sugars in the diet and a daily exercise program also help to control this form of diabetes.

ARTHRITIS

No review of conditions affecting aging, retired Greyhounds would be complete without mention of arthritis and joint deterioration that

Vitamin and mineral supplements can be useful in the treatment of joint conditions.

causes lameness, discomfort, and reduced mobility in Greyhounds in their senior years. Colder weather and cold living quarters often increase the risk. Lack of bedding on concrete floors or outside kennel areas can increase the risk of arthritis due to cold and dampness and has been reported to reduce a dog's life span by up to three to four years.

Aging, retired racers in particular have a higher incidence of degenerative arthritis, or osteoarthritis affecting toe, wrist, hock, and occasionally the stifle, shoulder, and lower back joints, often as a legacy of an earlier racing injury.

Degenerative joint disease results in reduced joint flexion and pain in weight-bearing limbs, often without obvious swelling of the affected joints. The severity of the arthritic change can be confirmed by X rays.

Various surgical alternatives are available to remove diseased cartilage and outgrowths of bone to assist repair of the joint surfaces. Rest and courses of anti-inflammatory drugs, either as topical creams or tablets, may be recommended. Heat-lamp therapy, liniments, pulsed magnetic field therapy, and, in severe cases, injections of cortisone into a joint to relieve inflammation and pain may be suggested, although cortisone eventually causes increased joint deterioration in many cases.

Recently, supplements of cartilage-protective compounds based on glucosamine, chondroitin sulfate, trace minerals, and vitamin C, as well as shark cartilage and perna mussel extracts have become popular. These provide a safe and effective nutritional means to assist joint cartilage repair and maintain the functional health of joints and cartilage. This will enable a retired Greyhound to have an active, relatively comfortable lifestyle.

Cold conditions can increase the risk of arthritis.

EPILEPSY

As the owner of a retired racer, you should be aware of the risk of epilepsy or nervous seizures; however, it is not as common in Greyhounds as in other breeds of dogs. Situations that cause over-excitement and nervous stimulation, such as race-day excitement, can trigger a seizure in young racing Greyhounds. In older Greyhounds, recurring epileptic fits, with nervous twitching, head nodding, stiffening of body muscles, and often collapse over a one- to two-minute period are either associated with earlier infection with distemper, a blow to the head, or a developing brain tumor. Keeping the Greyhound in a quiet, cool area following a fit and seeking veterinary advice is recommended if the "fits" occur more frequently than intervals of six to eight weeks or are particularly stressful on the Greyhound.

HEART DISEASE

Like many aging animals, Greyhounds can develop congestive heart failure. This is characterized by a reduction in activity and stamina, shortness of breath, and, in advanced cases, a moist, repetitive "fluid" cough when resting overnight. This is due to fluid buildup in the lungs as a result of a failing heart.

In severe cases, the animal may develop a swollen abdominal area due to fluid buildup, referred to as ascites, or, in human analogy, "dropsy."

Once again, diagnosis and treatment by a vet is recommended. In many cases, the Greyhound will be able to have a relatively active lifestyle

With good management, your Greyhound should live a long, happy, and healthy life.

with careful supervision and medication. Where infection with the common heartworm, *Dirofilaria immitis*, is diagnosed, specialized treatment may be necessary. This treatment may be conditional on the age of the Greyhound and the degree of congestive heart failure.

SUMMARY

Your retired Greyhound will provide you with companionship, loyalty, and affection, as well as be an active and easily maintained breed of dog for many years.

Regular vaccination, deworming, teeth care, a balanced and adequate diet without excess that leads to obesity, and daily exercise and coat care will ensure that your Greyhound enjoys a healthy lifestyle.

Even if an earlier racing career or a former uncaring home has left some health problems, your retired Greyhound will respond to your care. Remember, if your Greyhound has a wet, shiny nose, can wag his tail, maintains his appetite, shows a willingness to exercise, and has an interest in life, then he is a fit and healthy dog, and an excellent companion.